the
Secret
Ingredient
cookbook

the Secret *Ingredient* cookbook

125 family-friendly recipes
with surprisingly tasty twists

Kelly Senyei

HOUGHTON MIFFLIN HARCOURT
Boston New York 2021

*To my Grandmom
and my children.
Thank you for inspiring
me in the past, present,
and future.*

For information about permission to reproduce selections
from this book, write to trade.permissions@hmhco.com or to
Permissions, Houghton Mifflin Harcourt Publishing Company,
3 Park Avenue, 19th Floor, New York, New York 10016.

hmhbooks.com

Library of Congress Cataloging-in-Publication Data
Names: Senyei, Kelly, author.
Title: The secret ingredient cookbook : 125 family-friendly recipes
with surprisingly tasty twists / Kelly Senyei.
Description: Boston : Houghton Mifflin Harcourt, 2021. |
Includes index.
Identifiers: LCCN 2020034231 (print) | LCCN 2020034232 (ebook)
| ISBN 9780358353973 (hardback) | ISBN 9780358354260 (ebook)
Subjects: LCSH: Cooking. | LCGFT: Cookbooks.
Classification: LCC TX714 .S464 2020 (print) | LCC TX714
(ebook) | DDC   641.5—dc23
LC record available at https://lccn.loc.gov/2020034231
LC ebook record available at https://lccn.loc.gov/2020034232

Book design by Toni Tajima

Food styling by Kate Buckens

Prop styling by Maeve Sheridan

Printed in the U.S.A.

2 2021

4500822490

contents

acknowledgments

TO JULIO, MY HUSBAND: Thank you for believing in me and this idea since Day 1. You are my best friend, the ultimate business mentor, the most rational sounding board, and the most thoughtful recipe critic. Here's to a million years (and late-night bowls of ice cream) together. I love you forever.

TO JULIAN, EVAN, AND DEAN, MY CHILDREN: I hope in the years to come you will enjoy cooking from this book as much as I have enjoyed writing it for you. You are my everything and my forever inspiration. I love you more.

TO NONI AND DREW, MY PARENTS: I am forever grateful for my two biggest cheerleaders and self-appointed marketing codirectors. You are the most selfless, nurturing, generous, and supportive parents who have given me the courage to grow my passion into a career. I love you both endlessly, but I will still have to charge you every time you use the phrase "just a taste" without my permission.

TO ALISON AND KEVIN, GRANT AND BECCA, AND THE SIBERIOS, MY FAMILY: Thank you for all of your support over the years. I look forward to many more memorable meals together.

TO GRANDMOM: Thank you for instilling in me the importance of cooking for those you love, and for teaching me that it's always a good idea to have more than *just a taste* of doughnuts, pizza with pickles, and caramel-filled turtles. I love you.

TO LIBBY BECKER, MY SOCIAL MEDIA COORDINATOR: Building a company with you by my side has been a true honor, not only as coworkers, but as friends. Thank you for always keeping me on track, giving me a gentle nudge to swing for the fences, and making this Dream Team come true.

TO PETER CALLEY: It was a pleasure to have you by my side for the long hours of brainstorming, cooking, eating, tasting, and critiquing. Thank you for your thoughtful feedback.

TO STACEY GLICK, MY LITERARY AGENT: Thank you for believing in me and this book since our very first phone call. Your support has had a profound impact in shaping me as an author and businesswoman.

TO JUSTIN SCHWARTZ, MY EDITOR: I am forever grateful for your confidence in me as a writer and chef. Thank you for guiding me so honestly and thoughtfully through this process.

TO HOUGHTON MIFFLIN HARCOURT, MY PUBLISHER: Thank you for bringing this dream to life and for the support of every individual who has been part of the journey.

TO LIBBY, JOE, AND PATTI, MY RECIPE TESTERS: Thank you for cooking, tasting, and ranking your way through hundreds of recipes. I appreciate your thoughtful feedback and perfectionism.

TO ROBERT BREDVAD, KATE BUCKENS, TIFFANY SCHLEIGH, AND MAEVE SHERIDAN: Thank you for bringing my vision to life through your expertise in photography, food styling, and prop styling. I am incredibly thankful for your artistic contributions to this book.

TO THE JUST A TASTE COMMUNITY: Twelve years ago, we started a journey together that landed us here. I have loved watching our community grow and engaging with each and every one of you across so many platforms, from print to TV to the web. Thank you for your continued support in cooking and sharing the endless creations coming out of my kitchen. I hope this book provides more than *just a taste* of inspiration for your many meals and memories to come.

welcome!

The idea of recipes starring secret ingredients has been a cookbook concept I've dreamt about for the past eight years. It all began while tinkering with a basic chocolate chip cookie recipe, swapping out a portion of butter for cream cheese. The resulting cookies had soft, chewy centers that tapered off into slightly crispy edges. They were—and still are—the ultimate chocolate chip cookies (see recipe, page 224), and they've been baked and enjoyed by hundreds of thousands of loyal fans around the world.

From cream cheese in cookies and cottage cheese in smoothies, to mayonnaise in garlic bread and sour cream in whipped cream, I began experimenting with more surprising additions to classic recipes, and the results were (almost) all home runs.

Landing on the 125 tried-and-tested recipes in this cookbook was an exercise in creativity, flavor pairings, precision, and a willingness to taste things I'd never tasted before. There were some comical failures (pickle juice margarita, anyone?) and mind-blowing discoveries that have forever changed the way I cook.

Each recipe features a surprising twist—the secret ingredient—that gives it an edge and leaves people guessing. They know the recipe is delicious, they know it's not your average (insert recipe here), but they just can't *quite* put their finger on what takes it to a new level, be it in taste, texture, or presentation.

My goal wasn't to slap "bacon" onto every ingredient list and call it a day. Some secret ingredients transform a dish's color or consistency, others provide health benefits or time-saving shortcuts, and *all* elevate ordinary recipes into something extraordinary.

Extraordinary recipe results don't mean secret ingredients need to be unconventional, hard to find, or costly. As a mom of three little ones, I made sure the recipes in this cookbook are, first and foremost, family friendly. They are approachable, achievable, and practical, whether you're shopping at a farmers' market or at Walmart. In fact, if you can't find the ingredient on Walmart.com, you won't find it in this cookbook.

At the same time, I want to push you beyond the basics. There's a little something for every palate, every occasion, every holiday, and every life event. There are healthy breakfasts and indulgent breakfasts, vegan soups and meaty soups, 30-minute entrées and 3-hour entrées, kid-friendly desserts and adults-only desserts.

As you flip through the pages, I have no doubt that you will do a double take on many of the secret ingredients. Ginger ale in waffles? Sweet potatoes in queso? Strawberries in penne arrabbiata? Hummus in chili? You may be asking yourself, "Are these just gimmicks or actual improvements to recipes?" There are no gimmicks here.

This is a collection of recipes that have been rigorously researched, carefully written, strategically developed, and laboriously tested, retested, and then tested again. I made 91 trips to seven grocery stores throughout San Diego County and used 37 dozen eggs throughout the months of recipe development and testing. My goal was recipes that can be reliably replicated, time and time again.

I relied on a diverse team of cross-testers to ensure that replicability. Not a single one of them was a professional chef, and that was a very purposeful decision. I wanted to know how an average home cook would navigate being handed a recipe printout, with only the written instructions in front of them to guide the way. Their feedback inspired me to remove assumptions I had about techniques or ingredients and to get more specific with visual cues and descriptions. Case in point, the Savory Caramel Corn (page 65): I assumed the cook would remove any unpopped kernels before adding the popcorn to the caramel sauce. The cross-tester noted that this wasn't specified in the recipe, so their resulting snack included unpleasant, hard kernels. A simple clarification in the recipe means we can all now enjoy perfectly chewy caramel corn . . . and potentially avoid an unwanted visit to the dentist.

As a professional recipe developer, I'm often asked what inspires the inventive dishes coming out of my kitchen. My inspiration is as varied as the secret ingredients themselves, none of which was used more than once throughout the cookbook. I keep a firm pulse on the restaurant scene from coast to coast, studying menus online to look for trends and creative pairings suitable for home cooks to re-create with ease.

A culinary school degree and time spent in test kitchens shaped me as a professional chef, but I am still a home cook at heart. No matter how many thousands of recipes I've created, tens of thousands of dishes I've styled, and millions of photographs I've taken, at the end of the day, I'm not cooking in a restaurant; I'm cooking in my home. That translates to feeding a hungry husband and three growing boys multiple meals a day, plus snacks. So many snacks.

Like most kids, my boys take some convincing to try new foods. My success rate with getting them to not only taste but *enjoy* new foods comes down to one key strategy: They have to help make the recipe. Give them a bowl of broccoli, and surprise, surprise, the protests begin! Ask them to fly broccoli "spaceships" into the blender before adding a few other ingredients (including their favorite, olives) and pressing the "blend/blastoff" button, and suddenly, the whole family is sitting down to a single meal of Broccoli Pesto Pasta (page 129). But it's not all recipe wins all the time.

I fail on the regular in my kitchen, whether it's a flavor combination gone awry or a technique that just doesn't quite translate outside a professional kitchen. Those missteps have led to my greatest breakthroughs and successes. In the words of English poet William Blake, "The true method of knowledge is experiment."

As you thumb through the book, I ask that you be willing to experiment. Go outside your culinary comfort zone. Consider each recipe an adventure in your own kitchen. Have you ever made turkey burgers that included creamed corn? Most likely not. But one taste of the moist, flavor-packed patties and your turkey burgers will never go without this secret ingredient again.

So how should you approach cooking from *The Secret Ingredient Cookbook*? With an entirely open mind and an empty stomach!

To great meals and the best memories,

Kelly

essential ingredients

'm a big believer in a well-stocked pantry. No matter how much (or how little) space you have, filling your pantry and fridge shelves with essential items will make you much more likely to cook rather than reach for a takeout menu. When possible, buying in bulk will also help cut down on food costs.

Below is a list of ingredients that I always have on hand in my kitchen. I know not everyone is feeding four hungry males ages 6 months to 37 years around the clock, so don't hesitate to adjust these items to suit your family's dietary needs and space requirements.

PANTRY ITEMS

Kosher salt When it comes to salt varieties, kosher salt is king. It has an ideal crystal size and very pure flavor, making it perfect for seasoning every dish imaginable.

Large-flake sea salt Sea salt is great for finishing dishes. Its extra-large size adds salty crunch to savory and sweet recipes alike.

Black pepper Fresh is best when it comes to black pepper. Opt for a pepper mill rather than the preground variety to ensure salt's BFF is at its flavor prime.

Spices I could fill a swimming pool with my collection of dried spices and herbs, but the truth is, you really only need five to transfer your taste buds across multiple continents: garlic powder, ground ginger, ground cinnamon, ground cumin, and crushed red pepper flakes.

Extra-virgin olive oil If you're going to spend a few extra bucks anywhere, I highly encourage you to invest in a decent bottle of extra-virgin olive oil that's neutral in flavor. There are few things this healthy dip, dressing, and sauce can't do.

Balsamic vinegar While stocking any variety of vinegar is always a good idea, balsamic gets my vote for the most versatile. Mix it up in salad dressings, whisk it into marinades, or reduce it with a bit of sugar to make my go-to syrupy drizzle for veggies, galettes, and ice cream.

Flour I use all-purpose flour 95 percent of the time when cooking or baking—it can do just about anything. But if you're big on baking, I also recommend keeping cake flour on hand to ensure you're whipping up bakery-worthy sweets.

Vanilla extract It's the most-used extract in baked goods and also one of the easiest to DIY: Halve two vanilla beans lengthwise and scrape the seeds into a mason jar. Toss in the pods, then pour in 1 cup good-quality vodka. Seal the jar and let the mixture sit for 2 months, shaking it every few weeks. Voilà, a bulk supply of homemade vanilla extract that will last for years!

Baking powder Essential for making baked goods rise, baking powder only requires liquid to activate and work its leavening magic.

Baking soda Unlike baking powder, baking soda requires both a liquid and an acidic component to activate. Remember: "Soda" starts with an "s," which means it always needs something *sour* (read: acidic) to kick it into high gear.

White sugar Nothing fancy, nothing fake. Just regular ol' white granulated sugar.

Brown sugar You can't go wrong with either light or dark brown sugar. The only difference is the amount of molasses each variety contains.

Honey Honey is a great, sweeter alternative to regular sugar. Its syrupy consistency makes it a welcome addition to doughs, marinades, dressings, sauces, and beverages.

Peanut butter (or your preferred nut butter of choice) Beyond slathering it atop sliced bread, peanut butter is great for savory sauces, ideal for swirling into banana bread, and surprisingly complementary in a beloved stuffed appetizer (page 67).

Dried pasta Any shape, any size, any color, any flour. Dried pasta in your pantry means you're a maximum of 12 minutes away from a home-cooked meal.

Rice Pick your favorite variety, then keep it stored in an airtight container in a cool, dry place. Depending on the type, this starchy staple can last up to 5 years when stored correctly.

Tomato paste You can't go wrong with concentrated tomato flavor. I add tomato paste to my stockpot when I'm sweating veggies for soups and stews so that it caramelizes and intensifies into a rich, almost meaty flavor.

Hoisin sauce This sweet, tangy, umami-rich Chinese sauce is bursting with flavor and can be used in a variety of preparations, from glazes to dressings to dips.

Fresh citrus I always keep at least one lemon or lime on hand at all times. It's amazing how transformative a squeeze of fresh citrus can be in a dish.

FRIDGE ITEMS

Eggs They may be one of the most nutritious foods on the planet, but they're also one of the most versatile. Aside from the more than a dozen ways to cook eggs, they're also an essential item in baked goods, providing stability, structure, and moisture.

Unsalted butter Unsalted butter is essential for baking, but it comes in just as handy for savory preparations because it allows you to easily control the salt level of any dish.

Sour cream This is my dessert secret weapon and most common substitute in recipes requiring an acidic ingredient, such as buttermilk or yogurt. It lends a characteristic tang and provides endless moisture in baked goods.

Jam It's not just for toast! Stock up on a variety of flavors to use as the base for salad dressings (page 115), savory glazes (page 70), and fruit-filled frostings (page 239).

Fruit All the fruit, all the time. Pick your faves, prewash them (you'll be more likely to reach for a healthy snack if it's all set to go), then store them properly for maximum shelf life. Berries do best when they're washed, dried, and then placed atop a paper towel inside a container. Less moisture translates to less mold, which means less food going to waste.

Vegetables While fresh are great for snacking, frozen vegetables get my vote for mealtime MVP. My boys pop uncooked frozen peas into their mouths like they're popcorn. I don't know why, and I'm not asking!

Olives My boys' all-time favorite snack is olives—sliced black olives, to be exact. The salty brininess also makes them great for charcuterie boards, cocktails, pizza toppings, and quick-fix tapenades.

Cheese It's a food group in our house, so we're never without less than five varieties of cheese at all times, including shredded mozzarella, sliced cheddar, cream cheese, grated Parmesan, and crumbled feta.

Fresh herbs I've always dreamt of a thriving outdoor herb garden, but I've been blessed with not one but *two* black thumbs. If it can grow, I can kill it, so I always keep three types of fresh herbs on hand: chives, rosemary, and thyme.

my not-so-secret kitchen secrets

'I've cooked in dozens of kitchens across the country, from tiny New York City apartment kitchens to pristine test kitchens to my growing family's bustling kitchen. I've picked up countless tips—and learned even more helpful pointers through trial and error—over the past decade-plus of cooking professionally. These are my Top 10 kitchen wisdoms.

Secure Your Cutting Board

Day 1, Lesson 1 in culinary school is all about securing your cutting board to your countertop. While this may be a given to some cooks, others may not realize the importance of a steady workstation, especially when sharp knives are involved. To secure your cutting board, wet a paper towel with water, then wring out any excess liquid. Place it on the countertop then place your cutting board firmly on top. This simple tip guarantees your board will no longer slip and slide as you slice and dice with ease.

Proof Bread in the Dryer

My mom, Noni, is a master at all things involving baking, doughs, and breads. One of the first things she ever taught me in the kitchen was the best place to proof dough: your dryer! Run the dryer for 5 minutes, then turn it off. Transfer your dough (in a greased bowl) into the dryer, then close the door. The warm, humid, and dark environment is yeast's dream come true.

Quickly Ripen Bananas

Banana bread (page 31) is on the regular breakfast and after-school snack rotation at our house. No matter how frequently I'm whipping up a loaf, there are some weeks when I'm faced with barely ripe bananas, rather than their darkly speckled, extra-soft, and ideally sweet counterparts. To quickly ripen bananas to their peak banana bread–making stage, preheat your oven to 350°F and arrange the bananas on a baking sheet. Roast the bananas for about 15 minutes, or until they're black in color. Remove them from the oven and let them cool slightly before discarding the peels and scooping out the sweet fruit inside.

Understand Dry vs. Wet Measurements

There's a substantial difference between measuring ingredients in dry versus wet measuring cups. Spices, beans, oils, and vinegars can be clearly categorized as dry or wet, but what about sour cream, ketchup, and honey? As a rule of thumb, if you can run a knife across the top of an ingredient to level it off, it should be measured in a dry measuring cup. So sour cream, ketchup, and honey all fall in the dry measuring cup camp.

Quick-Freeze Meat for Perfect Slicing

Slicing and dicing slippery proteins can be a challenge, no matter how sharp your knife is. To get the cleanest, thinnest slices possible, wrap your meat of choice in plastic wrap and freeze it for about 20 minutes (depending on the thickness of the cut). The goal isn't to freeze the meat solid, but rather chill it enough to firm it up and make it easier to slice through. This technique works especially well when you want to very thinly slice steak for recipes like Beef Bulgogi Lettuce Wraps (page 179).

Wash Herbs in a Salad Spinner

When it comes to ingredient preparation, one of my least favorite tasks is washing fresh herbs, but a close-up glance at those tightly packed bouquets of parsley, cilantro, and dill often reveals an excessive amount of dirt and debris. The fastest, most efficient way to ditch the dirt? Give your herbs a very heavy rinse in water, and then toss them into a salad spinner. A few spins later and extra-clean herbs are ready for their close-up.

Zest First, Juice Second

When it comes to recipes that require fresh citrus zest and juice, always zest the citrus first and *then* slice and juice it. It may seem like a simple tip, but I forget this more often than I care to admit. I get so focused on extracting the juice from a lemon, lime, or orange that I completely neglect how difficult it is to then zest halved, juiced citrus fruit. Bonus tip: Room-temperature citrus fruits release more liquid than chilled fruit, so pop any cold citrus in the microwave for 20 seconds to get the juices flowing.

Use Your Serrated Knife

A chef's knife may be the most common cutting tool in the kitchen, but don't hesitate to ditch the popular kid for its saw-toothed alternative. Deciding on when to use a serrated knife is as easy as answering two questions: Is the food item slippery? Is the food item particularly hard? If you answer "yes" to either of those questions, chances are a serrated knife is your go-to tool. Always use a serrated knife with tomatoes, pineapples, butternut squash, and crusty bread.

Freeze Fresh Herbs in Olive Oil

Abundance of fresh herbs? Extend their freshness by chopping them up and sprinkling them into an ice cube tray. Fill each section with olive oil then cover the tray securely with plastic wrap and freeze it. Whenever you're in need of an herby kick to your dish (think pasta sauces, sautéed proteins, or veggies), pop a cube straight into the pan and get cooking. Not only do the cubes add flavor, but the prechopped herbs also save you precious meal prep minutes.

Give Your Rolling Pin a Guide

One of the keys to perfectly baked cut-out cookies is making sure all of the cookies are the same thickness so that they bake evenly and in the same amount of time. Rolling out cookie dough to an even thickness requires a lot of patience and careful precision. Not anymore! Place your cookie dough in between two sheets of parchment or wax paper then give your rolling pin bumper lanes by positioning two wooden dowels (the round handles of wooden spoons work well) on each side of the dough. Glide the rolling pin atop the wooden dowels and watch as the dough flattens out into an equal thickness all over.

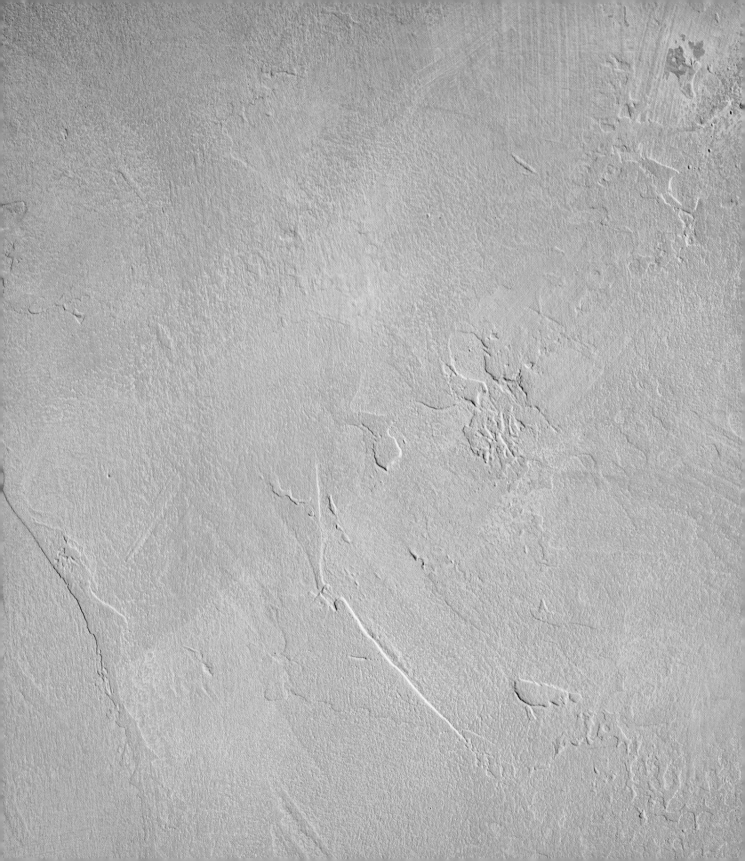

Breakfast

Berry Breakfast
Pastries (recipe,
page 35)

Shake 'n' Bacon Bites

It's the Great Bacon Debate: Cook it on the stovetop or bake it in the oven? For small-batch bacon, I'm all about sizzling up a few slices in a pan on the stove. But when it comes to bacon for a crowd, and especially *candied* bacon for a crowd, the oven is best. A sweet side dish is always welcome at my breakfast table, and this version in bite-size form tastes just as great served alongside eggs or pancakes as it does atop a salad or baked potato. Shake up your bacon in a bag with maple syrup, Dijon, and black pepper for minimum mess and maximum flavor in every crispy, crunchy bite.

PREP	10 minutes
COOK	35 minutes
Yield	*4 to 6 servings*

¼ cup maple syrup

3 tablespoons Dijon mustard

½ teaspoon black pepper

1 (12-ounce) package thick-cut bacon, cut into 1-inch pieces

Preheat the oven to 325°F. Line a baking sheet with parchment paper.

In a large sealable plastic bag, whisk together the maple syrup, mustard, and pepper. Add the bacon pieces to the bag, seal it, and shake until the bacon is evenly coated. Arrange the bacon pieces in a single layer on the baking sheet.

Bake the bacon for 25 to 35 minutes, rotating the pan once halfway through, until all of the fat has rendered and the bacon is cooked through. The bacon will crisp as it cools.

Remove the bacon from the oven, let cool completely on the baking sheet, then serve.

Vanilla Bean Drop Doughnuts

Secret ingredient

Greek Yogurt

My all-time favorite food has been the same since I was 11 years old: doughnuts. I even organized an unofficial New York City Doughnuthon in 2010, during which I trekked 5 miles while sampling nine doughnuts from three of the city's best bakeries. I've taken elements from each of my favorite fried carbs to create a simplified recipe that doesn't bother with yeast, proofing, or rolling, making these doughnuts totally doable any morning of the week. Protein-packed Greek yogurt does double duty, contributing both flavor and texture. It lends a subtle tang while ensuring your doughnut holes are moist, fluffy, and ready for dunking in the sticky-sweet vanilla glaze.

PREP	10 minutes
COOK	10 minutes
Yield	*6 servings*

FOR THE DOUGHNUT HOLES

Vegetable oil, for frying

1 vanilla bean (see Kelly's Note, page 20)

1 cup plain Greek yogurt

1 large egg

4 tablespoons unsalted butter, melted and cooled

2 cups all-purpose flour

¼ cup white sugar

½ teaspoon baking soda

½ teaspoon kosher salt

FOR THE GLAZE

2 cups confectioners' sugar

¼ cup whole milk, plus more as needed

2 teaspoons vanilla extract

● EQUIPMENT

Deep-fry thermometer

MAKE THE DOUGHNUTS Heat 4 inches oil in a large heavy-bottomed stockpot set over medium heat. Attach the deep-fry thermometer to the side. Line a large plate with paper towels.

Using a sharp knife, slice the vanilla bean in half lengthwise, then scrape out and reserve the seeds. Discard the pod.

In a medium bowl, whisk together the vanilla bean seeds, yogurt, egg, and melted butter. In a separate medium bowl, whisk together the flour, white sugar, baking soda, and salt. Add the wet ingredients to the dry ingredients and stir just until combined.

Once the oil reaches 360°F, use a small ice cream scoop (or two spoons) to add several 1-tablespoon scoops of dough to the hot oil, being careful not to overcrowd them. Fry the doughnut holes, flipping them as needed, until golden brown, 2 to 3 minutes. (If desired, first test fry one doughnut hole to determine cooking time.) Use a slotted spoon to transfer the doughnut holes to the paper towel–lined plate.

continued

Repeat the frying process with the remaining dough, returning the oil to 360°F between each batch. Set the doughnut holes aside to cool slightly while you make the glaze.

MAKE THE GLAZE In a medium bowl, whisk together the confectioners' sugar, milk, and vanilla extract until smooth. Add additional milk, 1 teaspoon at a time, to thin the glaze as needed.

Dip the doughnut holes in the glaze and serve immediately.

Kelly's Note * *Not ready to splurge on a vanilla bean? Substitute 2 teaspoons of vanilla extract for the vanilla bean.*

Sweet and Savory Egg Sandwiches

Strawberry
Jam

Peek into my kitchen any morning of the week and chances are you'll spy an egg sandwich. It's been my breakfast staple since college, when a bowl of cereal or a granola bar wasn't enough to power me through a snowy walk to class during Chicago winters. Here I've swapped out the more classic sweet-meets-savory pairing of ketchup and eggs for another perfectly balanced duo: strawberry jam and eggs. Slather the spread atop buttery brioche buns, then pile on the Swiss cheese, softly scrambled eggs, and salty slices of prosciutto for a 15-minute breakfast that's also become a dinner favorite at our house.

PREP	5 minutes
COOK	10 minutes
Yield	*2 servings*

4 large eggs

¼ cup dairy or nondairy milk

½ teaspoon kosher salt

¼ teaspoon black pepper

1 tablespoon unsalted butter

2 brioche sandwich buns

2 tablespoons strawberry jam

2 slices Swiss cheese

4 slices prosciutto

Crack the eggs into a medium bowl. Add the milk, salt, and pepper and whisk vigorously until the eggs are frothy.

Heat the butter in a medium saucepan set over low heat. Once the butter is melted, add the eggs and cook, stirring constantly, until the eggs are just cooked but still soft and custardy in texture, about 10 minutes. Remove the pan from the heat.

Halve and toast the buns. Spread the two top halves with the jam. Add one slice of cheese to each bottom bun, then spoon the scrambled eggs on top. Divide the prosciutto among the sandwiches, add the top buns, and serve immediately.

Fluffy Pancakes with Strawberry Syrup

Secret ingredient

Champagne

Champagne and breakfast go hand in hand, so why not give yourself *two* reasons to pop open a bottle of bubbly? Pour yourself a mimosa, then add a splash of Champagne to your pancake batter to ensure your flapjacks are fluffy and cloud-like in texture. The bubbles aerate the batter, which in turn puffs up the pancakes and lightens their consistency. Warm maple syrup would be a welcome accompaniment, but Champagne and strawberries—especially in syrup form—is a hard combination to beat.

PREP	10 minutes
COOK	27 minutes
Yield	*4 servings*

FOR THE SYRUP

6 cups sliced strawberries

⅔ cup sugar

¼ cup honey

2 teaspoons grated orange zest

¼ cup fresh orange juice

FOR THE PANCAKES

2 cups all-purpose flour

2 teaspoons baking powder

½ teaspoon baking soda

1 tablespoon sugar

¼ teaspoon kosher salt

1 cup Champagne

1 cup dairy or nondairy milk

1 large egg

2 tablespoons unsalted butter, melted

Cooking spray or additional unsalted butter, for greasing the pan

MAKE THE SYRUP In a medium saucepan set over medium heat, combine the strawberries, sugar, honey, orange zest, and orange juice. Bring the mixture to a boil, then reduce to a simmer and cook, stirring frequently, until the strawberries have broken down and the mixture has thickened slightly, about 15 minutes.

Remove the syrup from the heat and set aside to cool while you make the pancakes. (The syrup will thicken considerably as it cools.)

MAKE THE PANCAKES In a large bowl, whisk together the flour, baking powder, baking soda, sugar, and salt. In a separate medium bowl, whisk together the Champagne, milk, egg, and melted butter. Add the wet ingredients to the dry ingredients and mix just until combined but still lumpy.

Heat a nonstick skillet or griddle over medium heat, then grease it with cooking spray or butter.

Add ¼-cup portions of the batter to the skillet to form pancakes. Once bubbles form all over the surface of each pancake, flip them once and continue cooking until they are cooked through, about 4 minutes in total. Repeat with the remaining batter.

Transfer the pancakes to a plate and top with the strawberry syrup.

Caramel-Apple Cinnamon Rolls

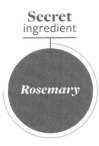
While apples and rosemary are nothing new in the ingredient-pairing department, you may be skeptical about letting this duo shine bright in a sweet breakfast classic like cinnamon rolls. I take my breakfast carbs very seriously, so trust me on this: Fresh herbs and tart apples tucked into the softest buttermilk dough is an a.m. slam-dunk. Balance the savory, tangy flavors with a silky-smooth cream cheese frosting and no cinnamon roll of yours will ever go herb-less again.

PREP	3 hours
COOK	25 minutes
Yield	*12 rolls*

FOR THE DOUGH

1 cup buttermilk

½ cup (1 stick) unsalted butter

⅓ cup white sugar, divided

1 (¼-ounce) package active dry yeast

4½ cups all-purpose flour, plus more for dusting work surface

1 tablespoon minced fresh rosemary

½ teaspoon kosher salt

2 large eggs, at room temperature

Unsalted butter or cooking spray, for greasing bowl and pan

FOR THE FILLING

2 cups grated peeled Granny Smith apples (3 medium apples)

4 tablespoons unsalted butter, melted

¾ cup packed light brown sugar

1½ tablespoons ground cinnamon

1½ tablespoons minced fresh rosemary

FOR THE FROSTING

1 (8-ounce) package cream cheese, at room temperature

4 tablespoons unsalted butter, at room temperature

1 teaspoon vanilla extract

1 cup confectioners' sugar, sifted

MAKE THE DOUGH Combine the buttermilk and butter in a small saucepan set over medium-low heat. Cook, stirring occasionally, until the butter has melted and the mixture is just below 110°F. Remove from the heat.

Add 1 tablespoon of the white sugar and the yeast to the buttermilk mixture. Stir, then let the mixture sit until foamy, about 5 minutes.

In the bowl of a stand mixer fitted with the dough hook attachment, combine the flour, rosemary, salt, and remaining white sugar. Add the yeast mixture and eggs and mix on low speed until the dough is smooth, 5 to 7 minutes.

Grease a large bowl with butter or cooking spray, then transfer the dough to the bowl and cover the bowl with plastic wrap. Set aside to proof in a warm, dark place until the dough has doubled in size, about 1 hour.

Grease a 13x9-inch baking pan with butter.

MAKE THE FILLING Place the grated apples in a towel and squeeze out as much liquid as possible.

continued

Lightly flour your work surface, then turn out dough. Roll the dough into a 14x18-inch rectangle. Brush the dough with the melted butter.

In a small bowl, whisk together the brown sugar, cinnamon, and rosemary. Sprinkle the mixture on top of the melted butter, then sprinkle the apples on top in an even layer.

Beginning at the long end closest to you, roll up the dough tightly into a log. Trim the edges, then slice the dough into 12 equal rounds. Place the rounds in the prepared baking pan, arranging them evenly apart. Cover the pan with plastic wrap and set aside to proof the rolls in a warm, dark place until doubled in size, about 30 minutes.

Meanwhile, preheat the oven to 350°F.

Uncover the rolls. Bake the rolls for 20 to 25 minutes, until golden brown and no longer doughy. Remove the cinnamon rolls from the oven and set aside to cool for about 20 minutes.

MAKE THE FROSTING In the bowl of a stand mixer fitted with the paddle attachment, beat together the cream cheese and butter until smooth, about 2 minutes. Add the vanilla extract and confectioners' sugar and beat just until combined.

Slather the frosting atop the cinnamon rolls and serve.

Kelly's Note ✳ *The rolls can be prepared a night in advance up through arranging them in the pan. Rather than setting the pan aside to proof the rolls, cover the pan securely with plastic wrap and refrigerate. When you're ready to bake, remove the cinnamon rolls from the fridge and let sit at room temperature for 1 hour before continuing with the recipe as directed.*

Baked Breakfast Flautas with Avocado Dip

Breakfast at our house is the usual early-morning circus for a family of five. My two toddler boys, clad in their choice superhero capes and cowboy boots, are flying around the kitchen island; the baby is busy trying to keep up; my husband is raiding the pantry for anything filled with protein that he can eat in 5 minutes or less; and our yellow lab, Wiley, is making his rounds, sniffing out stray blueberries from under the kitchen cabinets. Freezer-friendly, reheat-in-1-minute, protein-packed flautas are the answer to everyone's "What's for breakfast?" question. A cool and creamy avocado dip—reminiscent of the boys' favorite, guacamole—gets an extra (sneaky) protein punch from plain yogurt. The kids are happy to dip and dunk; my husband is happy for a hearty breakfast in minutes; and I am happy that my furry friend is on vacuum duty.

PREP	15 minutes
COOK	25 minutes
Yield	*4 to 6 servings*

FOR THE FLAUTAS

6 large eggs

1 tablespoon water

½ teaspoon kosher salt

¼ teaspoon black pepper

1 tablespoon unsalted butter

1 medium green bell pepper, diced small

1 medium white onion, diced small

1 teaspoon dried oregano

½ teaspoon ground cumin

½ pound breakfast sausage, casings removed

1 cup shredded Mexican blend cheese

12 (6-inch) flour tortillas

FOR THE AVOCADO DIP

1 large avocado, pitted and peeled

1 cup plain yogurt

½ cup loosely packed fresh cilantro leaves

2 tablespoons fresh lime juice

½ teaspoon kosher salt

¼ teaspoon black pepper

● **EQUIPMENT**
Toothpicks

MAKE THE FLAUTAS Preheat the oven to 425°F. Line a baking sheet with parchment paper or foil.

Crack the eggs into a medium bowl and whisk them together with the water, salt, and pepper. Set aside.

Heat the butter in a large skillet set over medium heat. Once the butter has melted, add the green pepper, onion, oregano, and cumin and cook, stirring, until the onion is translucent, about 5 minutes. Add the sausage and cook, breaking it apart with a spatula, until cooked through, about 8 minutes.

Add the eggs to the skillet and scramble until the eggs are cooked through. Add the cheese and stir until combined.

Divide the eggs evenly among the tortillas, placing them on the bottom third of each. Beginning at the bottom, roll the tortillas up and secure them closed with toothpicks.

continued

Arrange the flautas in a single layer on the lined baking sheet and bake until golden brown and crispy, about 8 minutes. While the flautas are baking, make the avocado dip.

MAKE THE AVOCADO DIP In a blender or food processor, combine the avocado, yogurt, cilantro, lime juice, salt, and pepper. Blend until the mixture is smooth and creamy. If the mixture is too thick, thin with water, 1 tablespoon at a time, until it is a pourable consistency.

Remove the flautas from the oven, then remove the toothpicks from the flautas. Serve with the avocado dip.

* Storing and Freezing Tips

To freeze the unbaked flautas, transfer to a sealable plastic bag and store in the freezer for up to 3 months. When ready to heat, preheat the oven to 425°F and arrange the flautas on a parchment- or foil-lined baking sheet. Bake the flautas until they are warmed through, about 10 minutes. Alternately, microwave the frozen flautas until warmed through, 30 seconds to 1 minute.

Whole Wheat Banana Bread

Homemade banana bread is a weekly occurrence in our house. It's so regularly on the rotation that I've dreamt up more than a dozen variations on my standard recipe, with every family member choosing their go-to loaf. My husband loves swirls of silky-smooth peanut butter in his bread, while my boys, not surprisingly, like all the chocolate chips that can be squeezed into a single slice. This slightly healthier spin swaps in whole wheat flour for all-purpose and olive oil for butter. The result is an incredibly moist loaf loaded with healthy fats, and because the oil is so neutral in flavor, it goes completely undetected, even by the tiniest of taste testers.

PREP	10 minutes
COOK	1 hour
Yield	*1 (9-inch) loaf*

Cooking spray

1¾ cups whole wheat flour

½ cup packed light brown sugar

1 teaspoon baking soda

½ teaspoon kosher salt

1½ cups mashed very ripe bananas

½ cup buttermilk

2 large eggs

¼ cup olive oil

1½ teaspoons vanilla extract

⅔ cup chopped walnuts or chocolate chips, plus more for topping

Preheat the oven to 350°F. Line a 9-inch loaf pan with parchment paper, then grease the parchment paper with cooking spray.

In a medium bowl, whisk together the flour, brown sugar, baking soda, and salt. In a separate medium bowl, whisk together the bananas, buttermilk, eggs, olive oil, and vanilla extract. Add the wet ingredients to the dry ingredients and stir just until combined. Stir in the walnuts.

Pour the batter into the prepared pan, then top with additional walnuts.

Bake the bread for 55 to 60 minutes, until a toothpick inserted in the middle comes out clean. Remove from the oven and allow the bread to cool in the pan for 15 minutes before slicing and serving.

California Breakfast Quesadilla

Secret
ingredient

Tater
Tots

Breakfast burritos are religion for this born-and-raised Southern California girl. My favorite fillings include chorizo, scrambled eggs, and Monterey Jack cheese, but the real reason anyone orders a traditional California breakfast burrito is for the extra-crispy potatoes tucked *inside* the tortilla. With this recipe, you can save yourself precious morning minutes by leaning on store-bought Tater Tots for the star filling and opting for assembling one quesadilla instead of burritos—its wedges make for easy dipping in homemade salsa.

PREP	10 minutes
COOK	15 minutes
Yield	*2 servings*

¼ pound uncooked chorizo, casings removed

1 tablespoon unsalted butter

4 large eggs

¼ teaspoon kosher salt

⅛ teaspoon black pepper

⅔ cup shredded Monterey Jack cheese, divided

1 cup cooked Tater Tots

1 small avocado, pitted, peeled, and sliced

2 (10-inch) flour tortillas

Charred Tomato Salsa (page 80), for serving

Cook the chorizo in a medium nonstick skillet over medium heat, breaking it apart with a spatula, until cooked through, about 8 minutes. Using a slotted spoon, transfer the chorizo to a plate, leaving all drippings in the skillet.

Reduce the heat to medium-low and add the butter to the drippings in the skillet.

In a small bowl, whisk together the eggs, salt, and pepper.

When the butter has melted, add the eggs to the skillet and allow them to cook undisturbed in a single layer, as if you were making an omelet. Use a spatula to lift up the edges of the egg, then tilt the skillet to allow any uncooked egg to run down under the cooked egg. Once the egg is cooked through, sprinkle ⅓ cup of the cheese on top, then remove the skillet from the heat.

Arrange one tortilla on your work surface and slide the eggs to the center of the tortilla.

Top the eggs with the chorizo, Tater Tots, sliced avocado, and remaining ⅓ cup cheese, then add the second tortilla on top.

Wipe out the skillet and place over medium heat. Add the quesadilla to the skillet and cook, flipping once, until golden brown and slightly crispy, about 2 minutes per side.

Transfer the quesadilla to a cutting board. Slice it into eight wedges and serve with salsa for dipping.

Kelly's Note * *The easiest way to flip the quesadilla is to first slide it onto a plate, then place a second plate on top. Invert the two plates and slide the quesadilla back into the skillet.*

Berry Breakfast Pastries

Secret ingredient

Cardamom

Store-bought puff pastry doesn't get the credit it deserves. With a few simple tricks, it transforms from a humble freezer item to a breakfast indulgence worthy of your local bakery's display case. While I'm all for making things from scratch, when it comes to puff pastry, store-bought is one shortcut I always take. These berry-topped beauties, which originally appeared on Just a Taste in 2016, have racked up hundreds of thousands of re-pins on Pinterest while simultaneously becoming a gold standard for Instagram-worthy brunch carbs. Ground cardamom lends an earthy richness to the tangy vanilla cream cheese filling and pairs perfectly with whatever fruit is currently hitting its peak—pears in winter, rhubarb in spring, berries in summer, or apples in fall.

PREP	25 minutes
COOK	20 minutes
Yield	*12 pastries*

1 (8-ounce) package cream cheese, at room temperature

2 tablespoons white sugar

1 tablespoon fresh lemon juice

1 teaspoon vanilla extract

2 teaspoons ground cardamom

All-purpose flour, for dusting work surface

1 (17.3-ounce) package frozen puff pastry (2 sheets), thawed

3 cups mixed berries

1 large egg, beaten with 1 tablespoon water

Demerara cane sugar, for topping (optional)

Preheat the oven to 400°F. Line two baking sheets with parchment paper.

In the bowl of a stand mixer fitted with the paddle attachment, beat together the cream cheese, white sugar, lemon juice, vanilla extract, and cardamom until combined.

Lightly flour your work surface, then unfold each sheet of puff pastry. Using a rolling pin, roll each sheet into a 10-inch square. Cut each square into six rectangles for a total of 12 pastries.

Transfer the pastries to the prepared baking sheets, arranging them so that they aren't touching. Prick the centers of each pastry several times with a fork, then score a ½-inch border around the edges.

Divide the cream cheese mixture among the pastries, spreading it evenly inside the scored section. Top the cream cheese with the berries.

Brush the egg wash along the edges of the pastries, then sprinkle the brushed area with the cane sugar, if using.

Bake the pastries for 15 to 20 minutes, until golden brown and puffed around the edges. Remove the pastries from the oven, let them cool for 5 minutes, then serve.

Skillet Sweet Potato Hash

Secret
ingredient

Beet
Greens

When it comes to a hearty morning meal, sweet potato hash gets my vote for the kind of stick-to-your-ribs sustenance that's guaranteed to power you through the day. The addition of beets, and especially beet greens, packs a healthy dose of vitamins and nutrients, and the beets themselves contribute to the hash's vibrant jewel-toned color. A splash of balsamic vinegar right before serving balances out the sweetness of the potatoes and cuts the richness of the breakfast sausage.

PREP	20 minutes
COOK	45 minutes
Yield	*4 servings*

1 pound sweet potatoes, peeled

½ pound beets with greens

1 tablespoon extra-virgin olive oil, plus more as needed

½ pound breakfast sausage, casings removed

1 medium white onion, diced small

2 teaspoons chopped fresh rosemary

1 teaspoon kosher salt

½ teaspoon black pepper

4 large eggs

Balsamic vinegar, for serving

Preheat the oven to 400°F.

Shred the sweet potatoes on the large holes of a box grater. Remove the greens from the beets, strip the leaves from the stems, and roughly chop the leaves. Peel the beets, then dice them into ¼-inch cubes.

Heat the olive oil in a 12-inch oven-safe skillet set over medium heat. Add the sausage and cook, breaking it apart with a spatula, until it is browned and cooked through, about 8 minutes.

Using a slotted spoon, transfer the sausage to a paper towel–lined plate. Remove all but ¼ cup of the drippings from the pan (or, if needed, add enough olive oil to make ¼ cup).

Add the onion and rosemary to the pan and cook, stirring, until the onion is translucent, about 5 minutes. Increase the heat to medium-high and add the sweet potatoes, diced beets, salt, and pepper. Cook, stirring occasionally, until the potatoes and beets are tender, about 20 minutes.

Stir in the beet greens and cook just until the greens are wilted, about 2 minutes. Return the sausage to the pan and stir to combine.

Using a spatula, make four wells in the hash and crack an egg into each. Transfer the skillet to the oven and bake until the egg whites are set, about 10 minutes.

Remove the skillet from the oven, drizzle the hash with balsamic vinegar, and serve.

Fruit Salad with Lemon Dressing (recipe, page 40)

Fruit Salad with Lemon Dressing

Secret ingredient

Vanilla Extract

It's hard to imagine fruit salad being anything more than ordinary. Cut up some fruit, toss it in a bowl, and call it a day. It's an easy crowd pleaser that checks a brunch buffet box. But once you opt to dress your fruit, I promise your opinion of this humble side dish will change. A mix of fresh lemon juice, honey, and mint gets a helping hand from vanilla extract, which lends a new flavor dynamic to whatever fruit looks best at your local grocery store or farmers' market. (*Pictured on the preceding pages, 38–39.*)

PREP	15 minutes
COOK	None
Yield	*6 to 8 servings*

1½ cups sliced strawberries

1½ cups cantaloupe balls

1½ cups halved green grapes

3 medium kiwis, peeled and sliced into ¼-inch-thick rounds

1 cup blueberries

1 cup raspberries

½ cup pomegranate arils

1½ tablespoons fresh lemon juice

1 tablespoon honey

¾ teaspoon vanilla extract

1 teaspoon minced fresh mint

In a large bowl, combine the strawberries, cantaloupe, grapes, kiwi, blueberries, raspberries, and pomegranate arils.

In a separate small bowl, whisk together the lemon juice, honey, vanilla extract, and mint. Add the lemon dressing to the fruit and toss to combine. Serve immediately or store, covered, at room temperature or in the fridge for up to 3 days.

Blueberry French-Toast Muffins

Secret ingredient

Coconut Milk

The morning meal in our house lasts anywhere from 30 seconds to 3 hours, depending on the day and, in all honesty, my kids' moods. While a leisurely breakfast sipping hot coffee and enjoying forkful after forkful of French toast sounds wonderful, that's not often our reality. Instead, coffee is unintentionally enjoyed chilled and French toast is served in finger-friendly muffin form. It's a surprisingly portable grab-and-go option any day of the week. Stale bread works best for French toast in all forms, but particularly well with these muffins. Big flavor comes courtesy of fresh blueberries, orange juice, cinnamon, and creamy coconut milk, making maple syrup a totally not-necessary addition.

PREP	10 minutes
COOK	30 minutes
Yield	*12 muffins*

Cooking spray

1 (13.5-ounce) can unsweetened coconut milk

2 teaspoons grated orange zest

½ cup fresh orange juice

6 large eggs

2 tablespoons sugar

2 teaspoons vanilla extract

1 teaspoon ground cinnamon

1 loaf French bread, cut into ½-inch cubes (about 12 cups)

1 cup blueberries

Maple syrup, for serving (optional)

Preheat the oven to 350°F. Grease a 12-cup muffin pan with cooking spray.

In a large bowl, whisk together the coconut milk, orange zest, orange juice, eggs, sugar, vanilla, and cinnamon. Add the bread cubes and blueberries and toss to combine. Divide the bread mixture among the muffin cups.

Bake the muffins for 25 to 30 minutes, until cooked through and slightly crisped on top.

Remove the muffins from the oven, then let them cool in the pan for 5 minutes. Using a sharp knife, cut around the inside edges of each cup to release the muffins. Top with maple syrup if you like and serve.

Bacon, Egg, and Cheese Toast Cups

Secret ingredient

Sour Cream

I lived in New York City for six years before moving back home to Southern California, and there's one thing I miss more than anything else the bustling city has to offer: a good ol' bacon, egg, and cheese sandwich. Most often served on a bagel, the B.E.C. (as the cool kids call it) was my morning commute staple. I've traded the bagel for puff pastry and turned the trifecta into brunch-worthy (and seriously party-friendly) bites, with sour cream lending a touch of creaminess and tanginess. Whip up a dozen of these easy, cheesy cups in less time than it takes to catch the 6 train.

PREP	10 minutes
COOK	30 minutes
Yield	*12 cups*

12 slices uncooked bacon

All-purpose flour, for dusting work surface

1 (17.3-ounce) package frozen puff pastry (2 sheets), thawed

8 large eggs

¼ cup sour cream

½ teaspoon kosher salt

¼ teaspoon black pepper

1 cup shredded cheddar cheese

2 tablespoons chopped fresh chives

Cook the bacon in two large skillets set over medium-low heat, draining the grease as needed, until it is almost fully cooked but still pliable. Set the bacon aside.

Preheat the oven to 375°F.

Lightly flour your work surface, then unfold each sheet of puff pastry and cut into nine squares each.

Add a puff pastry square to each cup of a 12-cup muffin pan, pressing it into the bottom and up the sides so the edges hang over the sides of each cup. (You will have six extra squares, which can be refrozen.) Place a slice of cooked bacon inside each cup so that the ends stick out of the cups.

In a large bowl, whisk together the eggs with the sour cream, salt, and pepper. Divide the cheese among the muffin cups, then pour the egg mixture atop the cheese, filling each cup three-fourths full.

Bake the egg cups for 18 to 22 minutes, until the pastry is golden and the eggs are cooked through.

Remove the egg cups from the oven and let them cool for 5 minutes before using a knife to loosen them around the edges. Sprinkle the cups with the chives and serve.

Cast-Iron Quiche

Secret ingredient

Hash Browns

If fancy is your forte, chances are you're a fan of all things quiche. The classic French tart stars a buttery pastry crust filled with a savory egg custard studded with any combination of meats, cheeses, and veggies. I always envision a slice of quiche served on the most delicate of china plates piled high with dressed greens. Because nothing says "fancy" like a salad for breakfast! Whether your occasion is an elegant baby shower brunch or a last-minute game-day potluck, this updated take on quiche is the answer to your feed-a-crowd prayers. Gone is the finicky pastry, and in its place is a good ol' bag of hash browns. The crispy potato crust is the perfect base for a flavor-packed custard starring an entire dozen eggs.

PREP	30 minutes
COOK	50 minutes
Yield	*8 to 10 servings*

3 tablespoons unsalted butter

3 tablespoons vegetable oil

1 (20-ounce) bag refrigerated shredded hash browns (about 5 cups)

1 teaspoon kosher salt, divided

¾ teaspoon black pepper, divided

1 (10-ounce) package frozen chopped spinach, thawed

12 large eggs

2 cups half-and-half

1 cup cubed cooked ham

2 cups shredded cheddar cheese

2 tablespoons chopped fresh chives, plus more for serving

Preheat the oven to 375°F.

Heat the butter and oil in a 12-inch cast-iron skillet set over medium heat. Once the butter has melted, add the hash browns, ½ teaspoon of the salt, and ¼ teaspoon of the pepper and stir to combine. Using the bottom of a dry measuring cup, press the potatoes into an even layer on the bottom and up the sides of the skillet. Cook the potatoes, occasionally pressing them as needed to compact the crust, until they begin to brown and crisp on the bottom, 7 to 10 minutes. While the potatoes are browning, make the filling.

Place the spinach in a towel and wring out as much liquid as possible. In a large bowl, whisk together the eggs with the half-and-half, remaining ½ teaspoon salt, and remaining ½ teaspoon pepper. Stir in the spinach, ham, cheese, and chives.

Remove the skillet from the heat. Pour the egg mixture on top of the potatoes, then transfer the skillet to the oven. Bake the quiche for 35 to 40 minutes, until the eggs are set and no longer jiggly and a toothpick inserted into the center comes out clean.

Remove the quiche from the oven and let cool for 15 minutes. Garnish with more fresh chives if desired, then slice and serve.

Kelly's Note * *Instead of store-bought hash browns, you can peel and grate 3 medium starchy potatoes (such as russets). Rinse the grated potatoes well with water, then place in a dish towel and wring out as much moisture as possible before continuing with the recipe as directed.*

Cinnamon–Chocolate Chip Scones

Secret ingredient

Zucchini

When it comes to coffee shop snacks, you're either Team Muffin or Team Scone. Up until my late 20s, I was a staunch supporter of the muffin movement and never understood the allure of the triangular pastry that was always dry and predictably crumbly. That all changed when I tackled this breakfast carb in my home kitchen with a tried-and-tested recipe from a popular baking brand. The scones were surprisingly light and tender and so incredibly moist. Six years and dozens of batches of DIY scones later, I arrived at my secret weapon for maximizing moisture: zucchini. The shredded veggie not only contributes to the consistency, but also serves a supporting role in highlighting the classic flavor combination of cinnamon and chocolate.

PREP	15 minutes
COOK	20 minutes
Yield	*8 scones*

1 medium zucchini

2½ cups all-purpose flour, plus more for dusting work surface

2½ teaspoons baking powder

⅓ cup packed light brown sugar

1 teaspoon ground cinnamon

½ teaspoon kosher salt

¾ cup heavy cream, plus more for brushing

2 large eggs

2½ teaspoons vanilla extract

1 cup chocolate chips

Preheat the oven to 400°F. Line a baking sheet with parchment paper.

Grate the zucchini on the small holes of a box grater. Using your hands, wring out as much liquid as possible, then measure out 1 cup loosely packed zucchini and set it aside. (Any leftover zucchini can be used later for muffins or added to banana bread.)

In a large bowl, whisk together the flour, baking powder, brown sugar, cinnamon, and salt. In a separate medium bowl, whisk together the cream, eggs, and vanilla extract. Add the wet ingredients to the dry ingredients and mix just until combined. Add the shredded zucchini and chocolate chips and mix just until combined.

Generously flour your work surface, then turn out the dough and gather it into an 8-inch round that's about 1 inch thick. Using a sharp knife, cut the round into eight wedges, then transfer them onto the baking sheet, spacing them at least 1 inch apart.

Brush the tops of the scones with cream, then bake until they are pale golden, about 20 minutes.

Remove the scones from the oven and let them cool for 5 minutes on the baking sheet before serving.

Green Machine Smoothies

Cottage cheese is one of the more polarizing ingredients in existence. And if I tell you to add it to a blender along with kale and spinach, I can completely understand your desire to turn the page. But hear me out on this one (and perhaps 124 other slightly strange ideas). Look past the texture to see cottage cheese for what it really is: a flavorless protein powerhouse. In addition to its health benefits, cottage cheese yields the most unbelievably creamy consistency without the added fat or sugar of more traditional smoothie ingredients. Intrigued? Confused? Tempted? There's only one way to find out . . .

PREP	5 minutes
COOK	None
Yield	*2 servings*

½ cup dairy or nondairy milk

2 cups lightly packed chopped kale

3 cups lightly packed spinach

2 cups frozen pineapple chunks

1 cup cottage cheese

1 medium banana, peeled

2 tablespoons ground flaxseeds

2 tablespoons honey

In a blender, combine the milk, kale, and spinach. Blend until combined. Add the pineapple, cottage cheese, banana, flaxseeds, and honey and blend until smooth and creamy.

Pour into glasses and serve.

Pumpkin Waffles with Maple Whipped Cream

Ginger Ale

What do Belgian waffles and Japanese tempura have in common? They both benefit from a carbonated beverage to aerate the batter and create a light, crispy texture. While tempura often uses neutral-flavored club soda, I've applied the same technique to pumpkin waffles using ginger ale. It lends subtle flavor, but more important, it allows you to skip the time-consuming step of separating and whipping egg whites to fold into and lighten the batter. Those extra few minutes can now be dedicated to something far more essential to pumpkin waffles: maple whipped cream.

PREP	45 minutes
COOK	10 minutes
Yield	*4 to 6 servings*

FOR THE WAFFLES

2 cups all-purpose flour

¼ cup cornstarch

½ cup sugar

2½ teaspoons baking powder

1 tablespoon pumpkin pie spice

¼ teaspoon kosher salt

6 tablespoons unsalted butter, melted and cooled

2 large eggs

½ cup canned pumpkin

1 cup ginger ale

¼ cup whole milk

Cooking spray

FOR THE WHIPPED CREAM

1½ cups cold heavy cream

⅓ cup maple syrup, plus more for serving (optional)

MAKE THE WAFFLES In a large bowl, whisk together the flour, cornstarch, sugar, baking powder, pumpkin pie spice, and salt. In a separate bowl, whisk together the melted butter, eggs, and pumpkin. Stir the pumpkin mixture into the dry ingredients (the batter will be very thick), then whisk in the ginger ale and milk.

Preheat the waffle maker, then grease it with cooking spray.

Add a portion of the batter to the waffle maker and cook until it is crispy on the edges and cooked through. (The waffles will continue to crisp as they cool. The cooking time will vary depending on your waffle iron and the thickness of your waffles.) Repeat with the remaining batter.

MAKE THE WHIPPED CREAM Combine the cream and maple syrup in the bowl of a stand mixer fitted with the whisk attachment. Beat on high speed until medium peaks form.

Top the waffles with the whipped cream and additional maple syrup, if desired, and serve.

Crunchy Coconut Granola

The first job I ever had was as a hostess at The Cottage, a small restaurant in my hometown of La Jolla, California. It was—and still is—a San Diego breakfast institution that's famous for its granola. So famous, in fact, that it packages and sells it in addition to making it the star of the breakfast menu. While the original recipe is a closely guarded secret, I did some reverse recipe development and trial-and-errored my way through many combinations of the ingredients listed on the back of the package until I arrived here: the best granola ever. The sugar in the sweetened condensed milk coats and caramelizes the oats, nuts, and coconut flakes, leading to the perfect balance of crispiness and chewiness.

PREP	10 minutes
COOK	30 minutes
Yield	*8 servings*

2½ cups old-fashioned oats

⅔ cup chopped pecans

½ cup sliced almonds

1 cup sweetened condensed milk

⅓ cup melted coconut oil

¾ teaspoon ground cinnamon

¾ teaspoon kosher salt

1 cup unsweetened coconut flakes

½ cup chopped dried pineapple, apricots, or cranberries

Preheat the oven to 325°F. Line a rimmed baking sheet with parchment paper.

Stir together the oats, pecans, and almonds on the baking sheet and spread into an even layer. Bake for 10 minutes, stirring halfway through, then remove the baking sheet from the oven.

In a large bowl, whisk together the condensed milk, coconut oil, cinnamon, and salt. Add the oat mixture from the baking sheet and the coconut flakes, tossing until the mixture is evenly coated.

Return the granola to the lined baking sheet and spread into an even layer. Bake the granola for 20 minutes, stirring halfway through, until golden brown.

Remove the granola from the oven, stir one more time, then let cool completely on the baking sheet. Once the granola has cooled, stir in the dried fruit and serve. Store the granola in an airtight container at room temperature for up to 2 weeks.

Snacks

Sweet and Tangy
Baked Chicken
Wings (recipe,
page 70)

Caramelized Onion Dip

Secret
ingredient

Soy Sauce

Few foods are as reminiscent of my childhood as sour cream–onion dip. It made an appearance at every birthday party, beach barbecue, and football tailgate, and it was never without its trusty companion, crinkle-cut potato chips. I've ditched the store-bought seasoning packet in favor of a homemade version starring *real* caramelized onions, along with garlic powder, chives, and the ingredient that brings it all to life with a punch of salty, umami flavor: soy sauce. Grab some fresh veggies for dipping, or go big with hot, crispy Homemade Potato Chips (page 77).

PREP	10 minutes
COOK	20 minutes
Yield	*6 servings*

3 tablespoons extra-virgin olive oil

2 medium yellow onions, minced (2 cups)

½ teaspoon sugar

¾ teaspoon kosher salt, divided

1½ cups sour cream

2½ teaspoons soy sauce

¾ teaspoon garlic powder

1½ tablespoons chopped fresh chives, divided

¼ teaspoon black pepper

Potato chips or crudités, for serving

Heat the olive oil in a large nonstick skillet set over medium heat. Once the oil is hot, add the onions, sugar, and ¼ teaspoon of the salt and cook, stirring, until the onions are golden brown and caramelized, 15 to 20 minutes. Let the onions cool completely.

In a medium bowl, stir together the cooled caramelized onions, sour cream, soy sauce, garlic powder, 1 tablespoon of the chives, the remaining ½ teaspoon salt, and the pepper.

Transfer the dip to a serving bowl, then top it with the remaining chives. Serve with chips or crudité for dipping.

Kelly's Note ∗ *For the best flavor, prepare the dip one day in advance and store it in the fridge, covered, until ready to serve. The dip will keep for up to three days when refrigerated.*

Noni's Soft Pretzel Knots

Secret ingredient

Everything Bagel Seasoning

If working with yeast seems like a daunting endeavor, this is a totally foolproof and satisfaction-guaranteed homemade bread recipe for you to try. My mom, Noni, has mastered the art of pretzel bread, achieving the perfect balance of pillowy soft centers with chewy, glossy exteriors. She transforms this basic dough into every shape imaginable, from twists to buns to the family favorite, knots. Toppings are just as diverse, ranging from classic salt to garlic butter to cinnamon sugar. But for the real wow factor, borrow a tip from the pretzel's carb cousin and shower your knots with crunchy, oniony everything bagel seasoning.

PREP	1 hour 45 minutes
COOK	15 minutes
Yield	*16 knots*

1¼ cups water, heated to 110°F

1 tablespoon sugar

1 (¼-ounce) package active dry yeast

3½ cups all-purpose flour, plus more as needed

1½ teaspoons kosher salt

3 tablespoons unsalted butter, melted

Cooking spray

½ cup baking soda

2 large egg yolks, beaten with 1 tablespoon water

3 tablespoons everything bagel seasoning, for topping

In the bowl of a stand mixer fitted with the dough hook attachment, combine the water and sugar. Sprinkle the yeast on top and let the mixture sit until it becomes foamy, about 5 minutes.

Add the flour, salt, and melted butter to the bowl and mix until the dough is smooth and begins to pull away from the sides of the bowl, 4 to 5 minutes. If the dough appears too sticky, add more flour, 2 tablespoons at a time as needed.

Coat a large bowl with cooking spray, then transfer the dough to the bowl and cover it with plastic wrap. Let the dough rest in a warm, dark place until it has doubled in size, about 1 hour.

Preheat the oven to 450°F. Line two baking sheets with parchment paper, then generously grease the parchment paper with cooking spray.

In a large stockpot set over high heat, whisk the baking soda into 8 cups water and bring to a boil.

Turn the dough out onto your work surface and divide it into 16 pieces. Roll each piece of dough into an 8-inch rope. Tie each rope into a knot.

In batches, add the pretzel knots to the boiling water and cook for 30 seconds. Using a slotted spoon, transfer them to the lined baking sheets.

continued

Brush the pretzel knots with the egg wash, then sprinkle with the everything bagel seasoning.

Bake the pretzel knots for 12 to 15 minutes, rotating the pans halfway through, until they are dark golden brown. Remove the pretzel knots from the oven and serve.

Crispy Crab Rangoon

I crave Chinese takeout on the regular, whether it's finger-friendly appetizers like egg rolls and pot stickers or sticky-sweet entrées like sesame chicken and honey-walnut shrimp. When it comes to re-creating these Americanized favorites at home, my goal is simplified, fresh, and fail-safe recipes that will have you ditching the delivery for good. Crab Rangoon is as simple as it gets. The unusual addition of curry powder catapults this recipe across *two* countries, blending Chinese and Indian flavors for the ultimate takeout-fakeout snack that's hot, crispy, and ready in 30 minutes. (*Pictured on the following pages, 62–63.*)

PREP	20 minutes
COOK	8 minutes
Yield	*6 to 8 servings*

Vegetable oil, for frying

1 (8-ounce) package cream cheese, at room temperature

8 ounces fresh lump crabmeat

1 tablespoon yellow curry powder

2 teaspoons minced garlic

1½ teaspoons Worcestershire sauce

24 wonton wrappers

Thai sweet chili sauce or sweet and sour sauce, for serving

● **EQUIPMENT**
Deep-fry thermometer

Heat 4 inches of vegetable oil in a heavy-bottomed stockpot set over medium heat. Attach the deep-fry thermometer to the side.

In a large bowl, stir together the cream cheese, crabmeat, curry powder, garlic, and Worcestershire.

To assemble, fill a small bowl with water and arrange the wonton wrappers on your work surface. Line a baking sheet with paper towels. Spoon 1 tablespoon of the filling into the center of a wonton wrapper. Wet your finger in the water, then run it around the edges of the wrapper. Bring the opposite corners together in the center and pinch firmly to seal. Repeat with the remaining filling and wrappers.

Once the oil reaches 360°F, add the wontons in batches and fry, stirring occasionally, until golden brown on all sides, about 2 minutes. Transfer the wontons to the prepared baking sheet, then repeat the frying process with the remaining wontons, returning the oil to 360°F between each batch.

Serve with Thai sweet chili sauce or sweet and sour sauce for dipping.

Crispy Crab
Rangoon (recipe,
page 61)

Three-Cheese Queso for a Crowd

Sweet Potato

Queso gets my vote for the most versatile and crowd-friendly snack in existence. It welcomes all forms of dippers, from tortilla chips to fresh veggies, as well as endless mix-ins (hello, chorizo and ground beef). Perhaps most endearing of all, queso is a no-fuss appetizer that's quite content keeping warm in a slow cooker for hours on end. My version has a touch of sweetness and a silky-smooth texture courtesy of a sweet potato, which no one has yet successfully identified as an ingredient in the dip. It's a great make-ahead option for feeding a hungry crowd at your next game-day get-together or Cinco de Mayo bash.

PREP	15 minutes
COOK	1 hour 5 minutes
Yield	*8 to 10 servings*

1 medium sweet potato

2 tablespoons extra-virgin olive oil

1 medium white onion, diced

2 cloves garlic, minced

1 medium jalapeño, seeded and diced

1½ teaspoons ground cumin

1 teaspoon kosher salt, plus more to taste

¼ teaspoon black pepper, plus more to taste

2 cups shredded cheddar cheese

2 cups shredded pepper Jack cheese

1 (8-ounce) package cream cheese

1 cup whole milk

Preheat the oven to 425°F.

Prick the sweet potato all over with a fork, place on a baking sheet, and bake for 45 to 50 minutes, until fork-tender. Remove the sweet potato from the oven and let cool slightly. Halve the potato and scoop the flesh into a bowl. Using a fork, mash the flesh well, then set it aside.

Heat the olive oil in a large stockpot set over medium-low heat. Add the onion, garlic, jalapeño, cumin, salt, and pepper and cook, stirring, until the onion is translucent, about 5 minutes.

Add the mashed sweet potato, cheddar cheese, pepper Jack cheese, cream cheese, and milk and cook, stirring occasionally, until the cheeses are melted and the mixture is smooth, about 10 minutes.

Taste and season the queso with additional salt and pepper, then serve warm.

Kelly's Note ✳ *Queso can be kept warm for several hours in a slow cooker on the low setting. Stir it every hour and thin it with additional milk as needed.*

Savory Caramel Corn

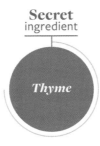

Secret ingredient

Thyme

Warning: I make popcorn with bacon fat. If you're applauding this revelation, then chances are we'd have gotten along just fine during my college days in Chicago. It's when my love affair with caramel corn began, all thanks to the city's iconic Garrett Popcorn. It ticks every box when it comes to snacking: It's crispy. It's chewy. It's salty. It's sweet. You can't ask for much more from the humble kernel . . . that is, until you work bacon and herbs into the equation. The result is an adult version of a childhood classic that's studded with candied bacon pieces and fresh thyme in every addicting bite.

PREP	10 minutes
COOK	50 minutes
Yield	*14 cups or 6 to 8 servings*

Cooking spray

6 slices thick-cut bacon, cut into ¼-inch pieces

¾ cup unpopped popcorn kernels

3 tablespoons minced fresh thyme

1 cup (2 sticks) unsalted butter

1¾ cups packed light brown sugar

⅔ cup light corn syrup

½ teaspoon salt

½ teaspoon baking soda

2 teaspoons vanilla extract

Preheat the oven to 250°F. Line a rimmed baking sheet with foil, then grease it with cooking spray.

In a large skillet set over medium-low heat, cook the bacon, stirring occasionally, until the fat has rendered and the bacon is crisp. Using a slotted spoon, transfer the bacon to a paper towel–lined plate, reserving the bacon drippings in the skillet.

Add 3 tablespoons of the reserved drippings to a large stockpot set over medium heat. Add the popcorn kernels and cover. Once you hear the first kernel pop, remove the pot from the heat for 1 minute. Return the covered pot to the heat and shake it quickly over the flame until all of the kernels have popped, about 5 minutes. Transfer the popcorn to a large bowl, discarding any unpopped kernels. Add the bacon and thyme and toss to combine.

Heat the butter in a medium saucepan set over medium heat. Stir in the brown sugar, corn syrup, and salt. Bring the mixture to a boil, stirring constantly, then allow the mixture to boil undisturbed for 4 minutes. Remove the caramel from the heat and stir in the baking soda and vanilla extract. (The caramel will bubbly vigorously once you add the vanilla.) Immediately pour the caramel over the popcorn mixture and quickly stir to combine.

continued

Transfer the popcorn to the prepared baking sheet, spreading it into an even layer. Bake the caramel corn for 30 minutes, stirring halfway through.

Remove the caramel corn from the oven, stir it one more time, then let it cool completely on the baking sheet. Once cool, break it apart into pieces and serve.

Kelly's Note ✳ *Caramel corn can maintain its freshness for weeks when it's stored correctly. A sealable plastic bag works great, but for the longest shelf life, store the caramel corn in an airtight container kept at room temperature.*

Bacon-Wrapped Dates

Secret ingredient

Peanut Butter

Before you turn the page or contemplate why I didn't just keep this secret ingredient to myself, allow me to explain. Bacon and dates are a duo for the ages. Almonds are the most common date filling. Almonds are nuts. Peanuts, while technically legumes, are still nutritionally classified as nuts. Peanut butter is made from peanuts. By the transitive law of logic, stuffing dates with almonds is the same thing as stuffing dates with peanut butter. Put simply: Sweet, salty, and savory food mashups just work, which is why dates, bacon, and peanut butter is the trio your appetizer lineup has been missing.

PREP	20 minutes
COOK	20 minutes
Yield	*8 servings*

24 pitted dates

½ cup crunchy peanut butter

8 slices bacon, cut into thirds widthwise

● **EQUIPMENT**
Toothpicks

Preheat the oven to 400°F. Line a rimmed baking sheet with parchment paper or foil.

Slice halfway into each date lengthwise to make it easier to fill. Transfer the peanut butter to a sealable plastic bag, then snip off a corner. Pipe about 1 teaspoon peanut butter into each date. Wrap each date in a piece of bacon and secure it with a toothpick.

Arrange the dates in a single layer on the baking sheet. Bake for 15 to 20 minutes, flipping them once halfway through, until the bacon is crispy.

Transfer the dates to a plate and serve.

Sweet and
Tangy Baked
Chicken Wings
(recipe, page 70)

Sweet and Tangy Baked Chicken Wings

It's hard to beat the crunch of deep-fried chicken wings. But when it comes to making wings for a crowd, manning a vat of boiling oil with tongs in one hand and a cocktail in the other takes a level of agility I am just not equipped with. If I'm hosting a party, I want to actually *be* at that party, not stuck in the kitchen. It's the oven to the rescue! Roasting the wings atop a wire rack allows the fat to drip off, which makes the skin extra-crispy. Toss them in a sweet and tangy hoisin-blackberry glaze and chicken wings are suddenly a fuss-free, low-maintenance snack for a party of two or twenty. (*Pictured on the preceding pages, 68–69.*)

PREP	10 minutes
COOK	50 minutes
Yield	*6 servings*

2½ pounds chicken wings, drumettes and flats separated

2 tablespoons extra-virgin olive oil, divided

1 tablespoon Chinese five-spice powder

½ teaspoon kosher salt

2 teaspoons minced garlic

1 teaspoon crushed red pepper flakes (optional)

⅓ cup hoisin sauce

⅓ cup blackberry jam

1 teaspoon toasted white sesame seeds (see Toasting Nuts and Seeds, page 105)

Preheat the oven to 425°F. Line a rimmed baking sheet with foil, then place a wire rack on top.

In a large bowl, toss the chicken wings with 1 tablespoon of the olive oil, the five-spice powder, and salt. Arrange the wings in a single layer on the wire rack, spacing them apart so that they aren't touching.

Bake the wings until they are cooked through and crispy on the exterior, about 45 minutes.

While the wings are baking, heat the remaining 1 tablespoon olive oil in a medium saucepan set over medium-low heat. Add the garlic and crushed red pepper flakes (if using) and cook, stirring, until golden brown and fragrant, about 2 minutes. Whisk in the hoisin sauce and jam and cook, stirring occasionally, until warmed through, about 3 minutes.

Remove the wings from the oven and transfer to a large bowl. Pour the sauce on top of the wings and toss to combine.

Transfer the wings to a serving platter, top with the sesame seeds, and serve.

Double Coconut Shrimp

Secret
ingredient

Coconut Oil

I was late to the coconut oil trend train. It didn't even become a pantry staple in my house until a few years ago when I discovered it was the secret to making the best hard-shell ice cream topping (page 263). From there, I started experimenting with it in savory forms, and that's what landed me here: Tiki party–style fried shrimp with double the coconut flavor. A dash of five-spice powder adds a burst of aromatics without being overwhelmingly spicy, while a dip into Thai sweet chili sauce rounds out the flavor profile of this globally inspired snack. (*Pictured on the following pages, 72–73.*)

PREP	40 minutes
COOK	12 minutes
Yield	*4 to 6 servings*

½ cup all-purpose flour

1 teaspoon Chinese five-spice powder

3 large eggs

3 cups unsweetened shredded coconut

Coconut oil, for pan-frying

1 pound large shrimp, shelled and deveined, tails on

Kosher salt, for seasoning

Thai sweet chili sauce, for serving

In a shallow bowl, whisk together the flour and five-spice powder. In a second shallow bowl, whisk the eggs. Spread the coconut flakes in a third shallow bowl.

Heat 1 inch of coconut oil in a large heavy-bottomed stockpot set over medium heat. Line a baking sheet with paper towels.

Dredge the shrimp in the flour, shaking off any excess. Dip the shrimp in the eggs, then immediately transfer to the coconut flakes, gently pressing the coconut onto each shrimp.

Once the oil is hot, add the coated shrimp to the stockpot in batches. Cook the shrimp for 2 minutes, then flip them once and continue cooking until the shrimp are pink and cooked through, about 2 minutes longer. Transfer the shrimp to the prepared baking sheet and immediately season with salt.

Add more coconut oil to the pan and repeat the pan-frying process with the remaining coated shrimp.

Serve the shrimp with Thai sweet chili sauce for dipping.

Double Coconut
Shrimp (recipe,
page 71)

Weekday Snack Mix

You may recognize tahini as the star ingredient in hummus, but this creamy sesame paste can be so much more than a dip. When roasted, tahini lends a rich nutty flavor to whatever it's joining forces with—in this case, your choice of cereals, pretzels, and nuts. I can eat snack mix by the bucketful, which is why I've ditched the butter and packed as many healthy ingredients as possible into this blend, including olive oil, whole grains, and turmeric, an anti-inflammatory powerhouse. The result is a crispy, salty, garlicky snack mix you can feel good about noshing on any day of the week.

PREP	10 minutes
COOK	45 minutes
Yield	*10 cups*

¼ cup tahini

¼ cup extra-virgin olive oil

2 tablespoons honey

1 tablespoon garlic powder

1½ teaspoons ground turmeric

1 teaspoon kosher salt

2 cups Wheat Chex cereal

2 cups Multi-Grain Cheerios

2 cups pretzels

1½ cups roasted cashews

1½ cups roasted, salted, and shelled pistachios

Preheat the oven to 275°F. Line a rimmed baking sheet with parchment paper or foil.

In a large bowl, whisk together the tahini, olive oil, honey, garlic powder, turmeric, and salt. Add the cereals, pretzels, cashews, and pistachios and toss to combine.

Transfer the mixture to the prepared baking sheet and spread in an even layer. Bake for 45 minutes, stirring every 15 minutes, until toasted.

Remove the baking sheet from the oven, stir the mix one more time, then let it cool completely on the baking sheet before serving.

Kelly's Note ✳ *To maximize the shelf life of snack mix, seal it in plastic bags or airtight containers and store it at room temperature. Because this recipe is made with olive oil, rather than butter, it will keep for up to 3 weeks when stored correctly.*

Sheet Pan Barbecue Meatballs

Secret
ingredient

**Orange
Soda**

If you're a fan of cocktail meatballs, chances are you're familiar with the famous slow cooker recipe starring frozen meatballs, chili sauce, and grape jelly. It has a devoted following online and in real life and became a fixture at my family's birthday celebrations as a crowd-friendly snack adored by all ages. I've swapped the slow cooker for a sheet pan, which allows you to enjoy meatballs from scratch in minutes, rather than hours. Orange soda lends a citrusy, sweet-and-sour-esque taste to the quick-fix barbecue sauce. Shape the meatballs into smaller sizes for snacking or go big to turn this appetizer into the main event.

PREP	20 minutes
COOK	20 minutes
Yield	*6 servings*

FOR THE MEATBALLS

Cooking spray

2 slices white bread

½ cup dairy or non-dairy milk

1 pound ground beef

½ pound ground pork

1 large egg

¼ cup minced scallions (2 scallions)

2½ teaspoons garlic powder

½ teaspoon kosher salt

¼ teaspoon black pepper

FOR THE BARBECUE SAUCE

1 cup orange soda

½ cup ketchup

⅓ cup packed light brown sugar

3 tablespoons apple cider vinegar

2 teaspoons Worcestershire sauce

1 teaspoon garlic powder

½ teaspoon smoked paprika

½ teaspoon kosher salt

¼ teaspoon black pepper

2 teaspoons cornstarch

1 tablespoon water

MAKE THE MEATBALLS Preheat the oven to 400°F. Line a baking sheet with foil, then grease the foil with cooking spray.

In a large bowl, combine the bread and milk and let sit until the bread has absorbed the milk, about 5 minutes. Mash it all together with a fork. Add the ground beef, ground pork, egg, scallions, garlic powder, salt, and pepper. Using your hands, mix together just until combined.

Scoop out 2-tablespoon portions of the mixture and roll into balls. Arrange the meatballs in a single layer on the baking sheet. Bake the meatballs for about 15 minutes, until golden brown and cooked through. (Larger meatballs will require longer cooking times.) While the meatballs are baking, make the barbecue sauce.

MAKE THE BARBECUE SAUCE In a medium saucepan, whisk together the orange soda, ketchup, brown sugar, vinegar, Worcestershire, garlic powder, smoked paprika, salt, and pepper. Bring to a boil over medium heat.

continued

In a small bowl, whisk together the cornstarch and water.

When the soda mixture comes to a boil, whisk in the cornstarch slurry. Boil the sauce, stirring occasionally, until it thickens to the consistency of syrup, 3 to 5 minutes. Remove from the heat and set the sauce aside to cool for 10 minutes.

Remove the meatballs from the oven, then transfer to a large bowl. Pour in the barbecue sauce, toss to combine, and serve.

Homemade Potato Chips with Warm Gorgonzola Dip

Secret ingredient

Fresh Mint

So much of my inspiration in the kitchen comes from dining out. This recipe is a mash-up of favorites from two restaurants that are 2,000 miles apart: The Winery in my hometown of San Diego, and Chicago Q, my go-to barbecue restaurant in the Windy City. We have the former to thank for introducing me to the surprisingly complementary pairing of gorgonzola cheese and mint, and we have the latter to thank for teaching me that homemade potato chips are absolutely life changing. Put it all together and you are an hour away from dunking hot, crispy potato chips into a warm, creamy gorgonzola fondue.

PREP	40 minutes
COOK	20 minutes
Yield	*6 servings*

FOR THE POTATO CHIPS

2 medium russet potatoes

Vegetable oil, for frying

Kosher salt, for seasoning

FOR THE DIP

1 tablespoon unsalted butter

1 tablespoon all-purpose flour

1 cup heavy cream

1½ cups crumbled Gorgonzola cheese

¼ cup freshly grated Parmesan cheese

2 ounces cream cheese

¼ cup sour cream

¼ teaspoon black pepper

2 tablespoons chopped fresh mint

1 tablespoon chopped fresh chives

● **EQUIPMENT**

Deep-fry thermometer

MAKE THE POTATO CHIPS Using a sharp knife or mandoline, slice the potatoes into ⅛-inch-thick rounds. Soak the potatoes in a large bowl of ice water for 30 minutes. Drain the potatoes and thoroughly dry.

Heat 4 inches of vegetable oil in a large heavy-bottomed stockpot set over medium heat. Attach the deep-fry thermometer. Line a baking sheet with paper towels.

Once the oil reaches 360°F, add the potato slices in batches, being careful not to overcrowd the pan, and cook, flipping as needed, until they are golden brown, about 4 minutes. Using a slotted spoon, transfer the chips to the prepared baking sheet, then immediately season with salt. Repeat the frying process with the remaining potatoes, returning the oil to 360°F between each batch.

MAKE THE DIP Heat the butter in a large saucepan set over medium heat. Once the butter has melted, whisk in the flour and cook, whisking, until the roux has thickened and is a pale golden color, about 2 minutes. Whisk in the cream and continue cooking until the mixture is scalding and has thickened slightly.

Reduce the heat to low, then stir in the gorgonzola cheese, Parmesan cheese, cream cheese, sour cream, and pepper. Cook, stirring occasionally, until the cheeses are melted, about 5 minutes.

Stir in the mint and chives, then transfer the dip to a bowl. Serve with potato chips for dipping.

Pan-Fried Feta with Lemon-Honey Dressing

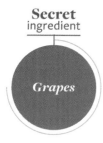
This is my take on traditional Greek *saganaki,* or fried cheese. A sturdy block of feta holds up well in a hot frying pan, crisping around the edges and softening slightly in the center without melting into a puddle. Cheese and grapes are a classic combination, but grapes aren't really the secret ingredient in this recipe, but rather *how they're prepared* that will have your guests reaching for a second serving. Blistered grapes add a pop of sweet, juicy flavor in every bite, while a drizzle of lemony honey with thyme rounds out the sweet, salty, sour trifecta.

PREP	10 minutes
COOK	30 minutes
Yield	*6 to 8 servings*

3 cups seedless red grapes

1 cup walnuts

4 tablespoons extra-virgin olive oil, divided

2 tablespoons fresh lemon juice

1 tablespoon honey

2 teaspoons chopped fresh thyme

⅔ cup all-purpose flour

1 (8-ounce) block feta cheese

Crackers or toasts, for serving

Preheat the oven to 425°F. Line a rimmed baking sheet with foil.

In a medium bowl, toss together the grapes and walnuts with 2 tablespoons of the olive oil. Spread the mixture in a single layer on the prepared baking sheet. Roast for about 25 minutes, until the grapes are blistered and the walnuts are toasted. Set the baking sheet aside.

In a small bowl, whisk together the lemon juice, honey, and thyme.

Spread the flour on a plate or in a shallow bowl. Dip the feta in water, then dredge it in the flour, shaking off any excess.

Heat the remaining 2 tablespoons olive oil in a small saucepan set over medium heat. Add the feta and cook, undisturbed, for 3 minutes. Flip it once and continue cooking until it's golden brown and the cheese begins to crisp slightly, about 3 minutes.

Transfer the feta to a serving plate. Top with the roasted grapes and walnuts, then drizzle with the lemon dressing. Serve with crackers or toasts.

Charred Tomato Salsa

When it comes to dips, it doesn't get much faster or fresher than homemade salsa. Blistering the tomatoes, garlic, and jalapeño under the broiler is a simple but substantial step that delivers big on the smoky flavor front. You may be surprised by not one but *two* unexpected additions: allspice and brown sugar. The former complements the charred veggies, while the latter completes the perfect salsa trifecta of spiciness, smokiness, and sweetness.

PREP	15 minutes
COOK	8 minutes
Yield	*2 cups*

6 medium plum tomatoes, halved

2 cloves garlic, unpeeled

1 medium jalapeño, stemmed, halved, and seeded

2 tablespoons extra-virgin olive oil

1 teaspoon kosher salt, divided, plus more to taste

¼ cup loosely packed fresh cilantro leaves

1 teaspoon ground allspice

¼ cup fresh lime juice

2 tablespoons packed light brown sugar

Position an oven rack 3 inches from the broiler and set the oven to broil. Line a rimmed baking sheet with foil.

Arrange the tomatoes, garlic, and jalapeño on the baking sheet and drizzle with the olive oil. Sprinkle with ½ teaspoon of the salt. Broil for 5 minutes, then flip the ingredients once and broil an additional 3 minutes, or until the skins are charred. Carefully remove the peels from the garlic.

Transfer the garlic and vegetables to the bowl of a food processor. Add the cilantro, allspice, lime juice, brown sugar, and remaining ½ teaspoon salt and blend until the salsa reaches your desired level of chunkiness.

Transfer the salsa to a bowl, then taste, season with additional salt, and serve.

Spicy Goddess Flatbread

Secret ingredient

Jalapeños

Step aside, Green Goddess! There's a sassier dressing in town, and she's cruising right past the crudités and joining the flatbread festival. This is my oversized take on trendy avocado toast that's meant for slicing and sharing. It stars a crispy crust, herby dressing, fresh veggies, and a hint of sweet heat, courtesy of candied jalapeños. These sticky rings pack big flavor and variable heat, but whatever you do, don't toss out the leftover jalapeño syrup. It makes for a mean margarita or a delicious drizzle atop fried chicken.

PREP	1 hour 35 minutes
COOK	7 minutes
Yield	*6 to 8 servings*

FOR THE CANDIED JALAPEÑOS

½ cup apple cider vinegar

1 cup sugar

2 medium jalapeños, stemmed and thinly sliced

FOR THE FLATBREAD

Cooking spray

¾ cup water, heated to 110°F

1 (¼-ounce) packet active dry yeast

1 teaspoon sugar

2 to 2¼ cups all-purpose flour, plus more for dusting work surface

3 tablespoons extra-virgin olive oil, divided

1 teaspoon kosher salt

Cornmeal, for dusting pizza stone or baking sheet

FOR THE SPICY GODDESS DRESSING

⅓ cup sour cream

⅓ cup mayonnaise

1 tablespoon fresh lemon juice

2 teaspoons Worcestershire sauce

1 clove garlic, chopped

¼ cup chopped fresh Italian parsley

1 tablespoon chopped fresh tarragon

1 tablespoon chopped fresh chives

1 medium avocado, pitted, peeled, and cubed

½ teaspoon kosher salt

2 Persian cucumbers, thinly sliced

1 cup microgreens

MAKE THE CANDIED JALAPEÑOS In a small saucepan set over medium-high heat, combine the vinegar and sugar and bring to a boil. Reduce to a simmer and stir in the jalapeños. Simmer the jalapeños for 5 minutes, then pour it all into a heatproof bowl and set aside to cool completely.

MAKE THE FLATBREAD Grease a large bowl with cooking spray and set aside.

In the bowl of a stand mixer fitted with the dough hook attachment, combine the water, yeast, and sugar. Let the mixture sit until it becomes foamy, about 5 minutes.

Add 2 cups of flour, 2 tablespoons of the olive oil, and the salt to the yeast mixture and mix until the dough comes together into a ball, about 5 minutes. If the dough is too sticky, add more flour, 2 tablespoons at a time, until it forms a ball. Lightly flour your work surface, then turn out the dough and knead it 10 times. Transfer the dough to the greased bowl and cover the bowl with plastic wrap. Let the dough rest in a warm, dark place until it has doubled in size, about 1 hour.

continued

Preheat the oven to 500°F. Dust a pizza stone or baking sheet generously with cornmeal.

Lightly flour your work surface. Turn out the dough and punch it down with your hands to deflate. Using a rolling pin, roll the dough until it is ⅛ inch thick. Transfer the dough to the prepared pizza stone, prick it all over with a fork, then brush it with the remaining 1 tablespoon olive oil.

Bake the flatbread for about 7 minutes, until golden brown and slightly crisped around the edges. Remove the flatbread from the oven and set aside to cool.

MAKE THE DRESSING In the bowl of a food processor, combine the sour cream, mayonnaise, lemon juice, Worcestershire, garlic, parsley, tarragon, chives, avocado, and salt. Process until pureed.

TOP THE FLATBREAD Slather the dressing atop the flatbread, spreading it into an even layer. Top the dressing with the sliced cucumbers and microgreens.

Use a slotted spoon to scatter the candied jalapeños on top (reserve the syrup for other uses). Slice the flatbread and serve.

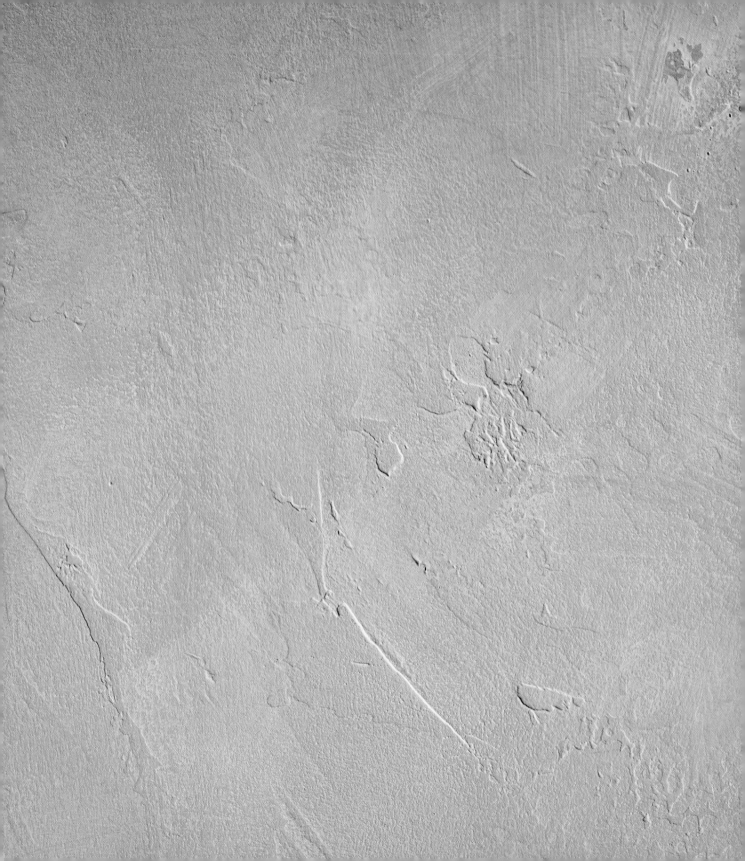

Soups
and Salads

Toasted croissants for
Kale Panzanella with
Lemon Vinaigrette
(recipe, page 107).

Tomato Soup with Mozzarella Toasts

Secret ingredient

Cannellini Beans

One of my all-time favorite meals in New York City is a bowl of tomato soup and a grilled cheese sandwich at Sarabeth's, a bakery/restaurant famous for its comforting American fare. The tomato soup is so velvety and rich thanks to a generous addition of heavy cream and milk. I've re-created this lunchtime combo, maintaining the creaminess factor, but without all of the added dairy and fat. How? Blending buttery cannellini beans into a smooth paste is a great gluten- and dairy-free way to thicken soups and stews while also adding protein and fiber. Because white beans are so neutral in flavor, they go undetected and take on the flavor of the tomatoes, garlic, and basil.

PREP	25 minutes
COOK	50 minutes
Yield	*8 servings*

FOR THE SOUP

3 tablespoons unsalted butter

1½ cups diced yellow onion (1 medium onion)

2 teaspoons minced garlic

3 tablespoons tomato paste

1 tablespoon dried basil

3 (28-ounce) cans crushed tomatoes

2 cups chicken broth

¼ cup sugar

1 teaspoon kosher salt, plus more for seasoning

½ teaspoon black pepper, plus more for seasoning

1 (15.5-ounce) can cannellini beans, drained and rinsed

FOR THE MOZZARELLA TOASTS

1 loaf French bread, cut into 16 slices

2 tablespoons extra-virgin olive oil

1 clove garlic, peeled

8 ounces fresh mozzarella cheese, sliced

Store-bought balsamic glaze, for serving

MAKE THE SOUP Heat the butter in a large stockpot set over medium-low heat. Once melted, add the onion and garlic and cook, stirring occasionally, until the onion is translucent, about 10 minutes. Increase the heat to medium-high, add the tomato paste and basil, and cook, stirring, until the tomato paste begins to caramelize slightly, about 5 minutes.

Stir in the crushed tomatoes, broth, sugar, salt, and pepper. Bring the mixture to a simmer, then reduce the heat to low and cook, stirring occasionally, for 30 minutes. Remove the soup from the heat.

Add 1 cup of the tomato soup and the beans to a blender, blend until pureed, and transfer to a large bowl. Blend the rest of the soup in the blender in batches, whisking it into the bowl with the bean mixture as you go.

Return the soup to the stockpot and cook over medium heat until warmed through. Taste and season with salt and pepper. While the soup is warming, make the toasts.

MAKE THE TOASTS Preheat the oven to 400°F.

continued

Tomato Soup with
Mozzarella Toasts,
continued

Arrange the bread slices on a baking sheet and drizzle with the olive oil. Bake until the bread is golden brown and crunchy, about 5 minutes. Remove the toasts from the oven. Cut off a small tip of the garlic, then rub it on one side of each warm toast.

Top the toasts with the sliced mozzarella cheese and return them to the oven for about 1 minute, until the cheese is melted.

Divide the soup into bowls and top with toasts. Drizzle with the balsamic syrup and serve.

Roasted Butternut Squash Soup

Nothing says "fall has arrived" quite like a bowl of butternut squash soup. It makes an appearance every year at our Thanksgiving feast and tastes just as great sipped casually from a mug as it does served in a porcelain bowl with crisped pancetta, sliced apples, and toasted pepitas on top. Raiding the cheese board for that much-coveted wheel of buttery Brie is what's going to earn you the title of Holiday Host(ess) MVP. The Brie melts seamlessly into the soup, leading to silky-smooth swirls of cheese in every bite.

PREP	20 minutes
COOK	1 hour 10 minutes
Yield	*6 servings*

1 (3-pound) butternut squash

2 teaspoons extra-virgin olive oil, plus more as needed

¼ teaspoon kosher salt, plus more for seasoning

⅛ teaspoon black pepper, plus more for seasoning

1 cup diced pancetta

3 medium Granny Smith apples, divided

1 cup diced yellow onion (1 onion)

2 teaspoons minced garlic

1 teaspoon ground sage

½ teaspoon ground nutmeg

3 cups vegetable broth

8 ounces Brie cheese, rind removed, cubed

Toasted pepitas, for serving (see Toasting Nuts and Seeds, page 105)

Preheat the oven to 425°F. Line a baking sheet with foil.

Halve the butternut squash lengthwise and remove the seeds. Arrange the squash, cut side up, on the baking sheet, then drizzle with the olive oil and sprinkle with the salt and pepper. Invert the squash so that it is cut side down and roast for about 45 minutes, until the squash flesh is fork-tender. Remove from the oven and set aside to cool. Once cool enough to handle, scoop out the flesh and set it aside.

In a large stockpot set over medium heat, cook the pancetta, stirring, until all the fat has rendered, about 5 minutes. Using a slotted spoon, transfer the pancetta to a paper towel–lined plate, leaving all the drippings in the stockpot. If needed, supplement the drippings with olive oil so that it thinly coats the bottom of the stockpot.

Peel, core, and roughly chop two of the apples. Add to the stockpot, along with the onion, garlic, sage, and nutmeg. Cook, stirring, until the onion is translucent, about 10 minutes.

In two batches, blend the butternut squash, apple mixture, and broth until pureed. Transfer the soup back to the stockpot.

Bring the soup to a simmer over medium heat. Stir in the Brie, reduce the heat to low, and cook the soup, whisking occasionally, until the cheese melts and the soup is warmed through.

Core the remaining apple and cut into matchsticks. Taste the soup and season with salt and pepper, then transfer to bowls. Garnish with the reserved pancetta, apple matchsticks, and toasted pepitas and serve.

Rotisserie-Chicken Tortilla Soup

I can think of 101 ways to turn an ordinary rotisserie chicken into an extraordinary meal, and chicken tortilla soup ranks at the top of that list. It's the ultimate meal-in-a-bowl that's hearty and healthy. If you aren't familiar with tomatillos, consider them the tartier, fruitier sibling of tomatoes. Charring them alongside poblano and jalapeño peppers results in a fiery flavor that's both bold and warming. In a rush? Swap out the DIY fried tortilla strips for store-bought, which lends the characteristic crunch to this Mexican-inspired favorite.

PREP	25 minutes
COOK	25 minutes
Yield	*6 servings*

FOR THE TORTILLA STRIPS

Vegetable oil, for frying

6 (6-inch) corn tortillas, cut into 2-inch-long strips

Kosher salt, for seasoning

FOR THE SOUP

1 pound tomatillos, husked, rinsed, and halved

2 medium fresh poblano peppers, stemmed, halved, and seeded

1 small jalapeño, stemmed, halved, and seeded

3 tablespoons extra-virgin olive oil, divided

½ teaspoon kosher salt

¼ cup chopped fresh cilantro, plus more for serving

6 (6-inch) corn tortillas, roughly chopped

6 cups chicken broth, divided

1 medium white onion, diced

2 teaspoons minced garlic

2 teaspoons ground cumin

1½ teaspoons dried oregano

2 tablespoons fresh lime juice

4 cups shredded cooked rotisserie chicken

Diced avocado, for serving

Crumbled Cotija cheese, for serving

MAKE THE TORTILLA STRIPS Heat 1 inch of vegetable oil in a medium saucepan set over medium-high heat. Line a plate with paper towels.

Once the oil is hot, test by adding one tortilla strip: It should bubble and begin browning. If the oil is hot enough, add the remaining tortilla strips and fry, turning, until golden brown, about 3 minutes. Using a slotted spoon, transfer the strips to the prepared plate and season with salt. Set aside.

MAKE THE SOUP Position an oven rack 3 inches from the broiler and set the oven to broil. Line a baking sheet with foil.

In a large bowl, combine the tomatillos, poblanos, and jalapeño. Drizzle with 1 tablespoon of the olive oil, sprinkle with the salt, and toss well to combine. Spread the ingredients in a single layer on the baking sheet. Broil for about 10 minutes, flipping halfway through, until charred.

Combine the charred vegetables, cilantro, chopped tortillas, and 2 cups of the broth in a blender and blend until pureed. Set the puree aside.

continued

Rotisserie-Chicken
Tortilla Soup,
continued

In a large stockpot set over medium heat, heat the remaining
2 tablespoons olive oil. Once the oil is hot, add the onion, garlic,
cumin, and oregano and cook, stirring, until the onion is translucent,
about 5 minutes. Stir in the remaining 4 cups broth and the tomatillo
puree and cook until warmed through.

Stir in the lime juice and shredded chicken, then taste and season with
salt and pepper.

Transfer the soup to individual bowls. Top with the tortilla strips,
avocado, Cotija cheese, and cilantro and serve.

Cheesy Corn Chowder

Secret ingredient

Tarragon

One of my earliest food memories is of my mom Noni's corn chowder. She made it every year on Halloween because it was the perfect hearty meal to fill us up before the rigorous candy-seeking expedition around the neighborhood. I've given this comfort food classic an adult makeover with the addition of fresh tarragon, an underused but ideal complement to corn in all forms. This is a 365-days-a-year soup in our house because it can be made with fresh or frozen kernels and also tastes great with a range of added proteins, from shredded rotisserie chicken to sautéed shrimp.

PREP	20 minutes
COOK	35 minutes
Yield	*8 servings*

6 slices thick-cut bacon, cut into ½-inch pieces

1 cup diced yellow onion (1 onion)

½ cup diced celery

2 tablespoons all-purpose flour

4 cups vegetable broth

2 cups half-and-half

2 medium russet potatoes, peeled and cut into ½-inch cubes

6 cups fresh or thawed frozen corn kernels

1 teaspoon smoked paprika

1 teaspoon kosher salt

½ teaspoon black pepper

8 ounces cream cheese, at room temperature

½ cup loosely packed fresh tarragon leaves, plus more for serving

1½ cups shredded sharp cheddar cheese

Cook the bacon in a large stockpot set over medium heat, stirring, until the bacon is crispy and all of the fat has rendered. Using a slotted spoon, transfer the bacon to a paper towel–lined plate and set aside. Leave 2 tablespoons of the bacon fat in the stockpot.

Add the onion and celery to the bacon fat and cook, stirring, until softened, about 5 minutes. Sprinkle in the flour and cook, stirring, for 2 minutes. Whisk in the broth and half-and-half. Add the potatoes, corn, paprika, salt, and pepper. Bring the mixture to a boil, then reduce to a simmer and cook, stirring occasionally, until the potatoes are tender, about 15 minutes.

Transfer half of the soup, along with the cream cheese and tarragon, to a blender and puree. Stir the puree back into the stockpot, then stir in the cheddar. Cook, stirring occasionally, until the cheese is melted and the chowder is warmed through, about 5 minutes.

Transfer the chowder to bowls, garnish with the bacon and additional tarragon, and serve.

Kelly's Note * *This recipe yields a generous amount of hearty chowder. If stored properly, it can last for months. Once the chowder has cooled, transfer it to airtight containers, then seal them and stash them in the freezer. To prevent the chowder from curdling while reheating, stir it continuously until it becomes smooth in texture.*

Beef and Farro Soup

Secret ingredient

Dark Beer

I have a confession: I despise beer. To this day, I have only ever taken a few sips of a cold one before turning to literally any other alcoholic beverage that's available. No matter how hard I've tried, beer and I are not buddies. So imagine my expression upon tasting my first *dark* beer, a frothy Guinness. It was sheer repulsion. But a funny thing happens when you cook with beer: it no longer tastes like beer. I use it to stew chuck roast, herbs, and veggies for a truly satisfying beef and farro soup that's easy to gobble up by the bowlful.

PREP	25 minutes
COOK	2 hours
Yield	*6 to 8 servings*

1½ pounds boneless beef chuck roast, cut into 1-inch cubes

½ teaspoon kosher salt, plus more for seasoning

¼ teaspoon black pepper, plus more for seasoning

2 tablespoons extra-virgin olive oil, divided

2 tablespoons tomato paste

1 medium onion, diced

2 teaspoons minced garlic

1 tablespoon chopped fresh thyme

2 bay leaves

2 tablespoons all-purpose flour

2 cups dark beer, such as Guinness

8 cups beef broth

1½ cups uncooked farro

3 cups chopped kale

Freshly grated Parmesan cheese, for serving

Chopped fresh Italian parsley, for serving

Season the beef with the salt and pepper. In a large stockpot set over medium heat, heat 1 tablespoon of the olive oil. Once the oil is hot, add half the beef (to avoid crowding) and cook, stirring occasionally, until browned on all sides, about 5 minutes. Use a slotted spoon to transfer the beef to a bowl. Repeat to brown the remaining beef. Leave all of the drippings in the stockpot.

Add the remaining 1 tablespoon olive oil to the stockpot, then add the tomato paste, onion, garlic, thyme, and bay leaves and cook, stirring, until the tomato paste begins to caramelize, about 3 minutes. Sprinkle in the flour and cook, stirring, for 1 minute. Add the beer to deglaze, using a wooden spoon to scrape up all the brown bits from the bottom of the stockpot.

Return the beef to the stockpot, then add the broth. Bring the mixture to a boil and reduce to a simmer. Cover the stockpot and simmer the soup for 1 hour.

Add the farro, cover the stockpot, and cook until the farro is tender, about 30 minutes. Add the kale and cook for an additional 5 minutes. Remove the bay leaves, then taste and season the soup with salt and pepper.

Transfer the soup to bowls, garnish with Parmesan cheese and parsley, and serve.

Curried Red Lentil Soup

Pear

I'm a meat and cheese kind of girl, so I find it ironic that one of my all-time favorite soups happens to be not only vegetarian, but also vegan. This creamy soup gets its silky-smooth consistency from a quick pulse in the blender. While tender lentils are the centerpiece here, fresh pears sautéed with garlic, ginger, and curry powder end up stealing the show. The soup leans closest to traditional Indian dal, a dish consisting of slow-simmered pulses (lentils, peas, and beans), so it's only fitting to accompany your bowl with wedges of warm naan for dipping and dunking.

PREP	25 minutes
COOK	35 minutes
Yield	*6 servings*

2 tablespoons extra-virgin olive oil

1 cup diced white onion (1 onion)

½ cup diced peeled carrot

2 medium pears, peeled, cored, and diced (see Kelly's Note)

½ teaspoon kosher salt, plus more for seasoning

2 teaspoons minced garlic

1 tablespoon minced fresh ginger

1 tablespoon yellow curry powder

¼ teaspoon cayenne pepper

2 cups red lentils

6 cups vegetable broth

2 tablespoons fresh lime juice

Chopped fresh cilantro, for garnish

Naan, for serving

Heat the olive oil in a large stockpot set over medium heat. Once the oil is hot, add the onion, carrot, pears, and salt. Cook, stirring, until the ingredients have softened, about 10 minutes. Stir in the garlic, ginger, curry powder, and cayenne and continue cooking for an additional 3 minutes.

Add the lentils and broth. Bring the mixture to a boil, then reduce to a simmer and cook until the lentils are soft, about 20 minutes.

Transfer the soup to a blender in batches and puree until smooth. Return the soup to the stockpot, then stir in the lime juice. Taste and season the soup with salt.

Transfer the soup to bowls, top with cilantro, and serve with naan for dipping.

Kelly's Note * *If pears aren't in season, swap in any variety of red apple to achieve the same subtle sweetness.*

Soupy Thai Chicken Noodles

What do you get when an American classic like chicken noodle soup and a Thai favorite like *tom kha gai* join forces? The most flavor-packed, warm-your-soul bowl of Soupy Thai Chicken Noodles. I've borrowed the hot and sour flavor of Thailand's treasured coconut soup and paired it with tender cubes of chicken thighs, rice noodles, and the slew of spices that are packed into every tablespoon of red curry paste. Minced fresh garlic and ginger make this soup the ultimate cold- and flu-fighting machine, no matter the season. (*Pictured on the following pages, 100–101.*)

PREP	40 minutes
COOK	35 minutes
Yield	*6 servings*

1 tablespoon vegetable oil

1 cup shredded peeled carrots

½ cup chopped scallions, plus more for garnish (3 scallions)

1 tablespoon minced garlic

2 teaspoons minced fresh ginger

2 tablespoons Thai red curry paste

2 tablespoons soy sauce

1 pound boneless skinless chicken thighs, cut into 1-inch cubes

4 cups chicken broth

2 (15-ounce) cans unsweetened coconut milk

⅓ cup fresh lime juice

¼ cup packed brown sugar

16 ounces rice noodles, cooked per package directions

Kosher salt, for seasoning

Chopped fresh cilantro, for garnish

In a large stockpot set over medium heat, heat the vegetable oil. Once the oil is hot, add the carrots, scallions, garlic, ginger, and curry paste and cook, stirring, until fragrant and the garlic is golden, 3 to 5 minutes.

Push the veggies to one side of the pan and add the soy sauce, then the chicken cubes in a single layer. Cook, undisturbed, for 3 minutes. Flip the chicken cubes once and cook for an additional 2 minutes.

Add the broth and bring the soup to a simmer. Reduce the heat to medium-low and simmer for 20 minutes. Stir in the coconut milk, lime juice, and brown sugar and cook until warmed through.

Add the cooked noodles, then taste and season with salt. Transfer the soup to bowls, garnish with cilantro and scallions, and serve.

Soupy Thai
Chicken Noodles
(recipe, page 99)

Caprese Antipasto Salad

Secret ingredient

Fried Mozzarella

I can make an entire meal out of antipasto, the traditional Italian pre-pasta course featuring cured meats, various cheeses, and pickled veggies. Bite-size balls of mozzarella are my go-to, especially when tucked inside slices of salami. But if there's one thing I know about assembling the ultimate antipasto lineup, it's that cheese is good, but *fried* cheese is even better. Imagine a single-bite version of mozzarella sticks, starring a crunchy breadcrumb coating that gives way to a hot and cheesy center. Pile the fried cheese balls atop a bed of fresh veggies for the perfect harmony of warm, cool, creamy, and crunchy elements in every bite.

PREP	25 minutes
COOK	6 minutes
Yield	*4 servings*

FOR THE VINAIGRETTE

¼ cup red wine vinegar

2 teaspoons honey

1 tablespoon minced shallot

1 teaspoon dried basil

½ teaspoon kosher salt

¼ teaspoon black pepper

¼ cup extra-virgin olive oil

FOR THE SALAD

4 cups arugula

1 cup diced salami

½ cup jarred sliced pepperoncini

1 cup marinated artichoke hearts, drained and quartered

2 cups halved cherry tomatoes

½ cup sliced black olives

FOR THE FRIED MOZZARELLA

Vegetable oil, for frying

1 (7-ounce) package mini mozzarella balls (bocconcini or ciliegine)

⅓ cup all-purpose flour

2 large eggs

⅔ cup breadcrumbs

Kosher salt, to taste

• **EQUIPMENT**

Deep-fry thermometer

MAKE THE VINAIGRETTE In a small bowl, whisk together the vinegar, honey, shallot, basil, salt, and pepper. While whisking, stream in the olive oil and continue whisking until emulsified. Set the vinaigrette aside.

MAKE THE SALAD In a large bowl, toss together the arugula, salami, pepperoncini, artichoke hearts, cherry tomatoes, and olives.

FRY THE MOZZARELLA BALLS In a heavy-bottomed stockpot set over medium heat, add 3 inches vegetable oil. Attach a deep-fry thermometer to the side. Line a plate with paper towels.

Remove the mozzarella balls from the package and thoroughly dry them. Spread the flour in a shallow dish. In a second shallow dish, whisk together the eggs. Spread the breadcrumbs in a third shallow dish.

Dredge the mozzarella balls in the flour, shaking off any excess, then dip them in the eggs and then into the breadcrumbs, coating them all over.

Once the oil reaches 360°F, add the mozzarella balls in batches (do not overcrowd) and fry, turning

continued

Caprese
Antipasto Salad,
continued

occasionally, until golden brown all over, about 2 minutes. Using a slotted spoon, transfer the mozzarella balls to the paper towel–lined plate and immediately season with salt. Repeat the frying process with the remaining mozzarella balls, returning the oil to 360°F between each batch.

Toss the salad with the vinaigrette and serve topped with the fried mozzarella balls.

Super Greens Salad with Balsamic Vinaigrette

Secret ingredient

Coffee

Quick poll: You're standing in front of a salad bar and have 5 minutes to assemble your dream salad. What ingredients would you choose? My bowl would be filled to the brim with a mix of super greens, cucumbers, pungent cheese, fresh and dried fruits, nuts, and, to top it all off, a balsamic vinaigrette that is both flavorful and functional (hello, much-needed afternoon caffeine kick). Coffee and balsamic may seem like the odd couple, but the roasted richness of the brew complements the bitterness of the vinegar and balances the sweetness of the honey to create a mix of flavors that energetically dresses up any bowl of greens.

PREP	15 minutes
COOK	None
Yield	*4 servings*

FOR THE SALAD

4 cups spinach

4 cups shredded kale

1 medium cucumber, diced

1 medium Granny Smith apple, cored and cut into matchsticks

⅔ cup blue cheese crumbles

½ cup slivered almonds, toasted (see Note)

¾ cup dried cranberries

FOR THE VINAIGRETTE

2 tablespoons balsamic vinegar

1 tablespoon brewed coffee

1 tablespoon honey

¼ teaspoon kosher salt

⅛ teaspoon black pepper

½ cup extra-virgin olive oil

MAKE THE SALAD In a large bowl, combine the spinach, kale, cucumber, apple, blue cheese, almonds, and cranberries.

MAKE THE DRESSING In a medium bowl, whisk together the balsamic vinegar, coffee, honey, salt, and pepper. While whisking, stream in the olive oil and continue whisking until the vinaigrette is emulsified.

Pour the vinaigrette over the salad. Toss to combine and serve.

* Toasting Nuts and Seeds

To toast any variety of shelled nuts or seeds, cook them in a skillet over low heat, shaking the skillet regularly, until the nuts or seeds are toasted and fragrant. The cook time will vary based on the size and type of nut or seed, but don't step away from the skillet, as they can burn very quickly.

Kale Panzanella with Lemon Vinaigrette

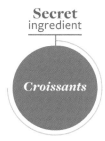

Secret ingredient

Croissants

If your idea of a salad is croutons with a side of greens, then this panzanella (aka Tuscan bread salad) is for you. While panzanella is traditionally made with crusty bread, I've upped the carb factor with hand-torn buttery croissants. This is your chance to put those stale pastries to good use, because dry bread works best when it comes to absorbing liquids. To maximize flavor and texture, toast the croissant pieces in the oven to ensure they're crisped and primed for soaking up puddles of the lemon-Dijon vinaigrette.

PREP	20 minutes
COOK	10 minutes
Yield	*4 servings*

FOR THE PANZANELLA

4 medium croissants, torn into 1-inch pieces

2 tablespoons extra-virgin olive oil

½ teaspoon kosher salt

¼ teaspoon black pepper

4 cups shredded kale

2 cups halved cherry tomatoes

1 medium orange bell pepper, diced

½ cup sliced red onion

2 cups diced cucumber

FOR THE VINAIGRETTE

½ teaspoon grated lemon zest

5 tablespoons fresh lemon juice

1 tablespoon Dijon mustard

1 teaspoon minced garlic

2 teaspoons honey

½ teaspoon kosher salt

¼ teaspoon black pepper

½ cup extra-virgin olive oil

MAKE THE PANZANELLA Preheat the oven to 375°F. Line a baking sheet with parchment paper.

In a large bowl, toss the croissant pieces with the olive oil, salt, and pepper. Transfer them to the baking sheet and bake for 10 minutes, tossing them halfway through, until crisped.

Transfer the croissant pieces to a large bowl, then stir in the kale, tomatoes, bell pepper, red onion, and cucumber.

MAKE THE VINAIGRETTE In a small bowl, whisk together the lemon zest, lemon juice, mustard, garlic, honey, salt, and pepper. While whisking, stream in the olive oil and continue whisking until emulsified.

Pour the dressing over the panzanella, toss to combine, and serve.

Caesar Pasta Salad
(recipe, page 110)

Caesar Pasta Salad

A variation of this recipe first appeared on Just a Taste in 2019, and within a few months had racked up hundreds of thousands of views and an equal number of fans on Pinterest and Instagram. While pasta salad popularity tends to skew toward summer months, this five-star-rated recipe has become a year-round hit. I've updated it to include omega-rich avocado in place of eggs, which yields an even creamier consistency than the classic dressing. It's loved by many not only as a healthy dressing for crisp greens and pasta, but also as a dip for veggies, pretzels, pita bread, and all other dunkable items. (*Pictured on page 109.*)

PREP	10 minutes
COOK	10 minutes
Yield	*4 to 6 servings*

FOR THE DRESSING

¼ cup Dijon mustard

¼ cup fresh lemon juice

2 tablespoons Worcestershire sauce

2 small avocados, pitted and peeled

1 tablespoon minced garlic

2 teaspoons anchovy paste

½ cup extra-virgin olive oil

½ cup finely grated Parmesan cheese, plus more for serving

¼ teaspoon black pepper

FOR THE SALAD

8 ounces uncooked pasta, such as rotini or penne

2 hearts of romaine

1½ cups croutons

MAKE THE DRESSING In a blender, combine the mustard, lemon juice, Worcestershire, avocados, garlic, and anchovy paste. Pulse until blended and then, with the blender running, stream in the olive oil. Transfer the dressing to a bowl and stir in the Parmesan cheese and pepper.

MAKE THE SALAD Bring a large pot of salted water to a boil. Add the pasta and cook until al dente, about 10 minutes, or according to package directions. Drain the pasta. Transfer to a large serving bowl and let cool slightly.

Cut the romaine hearts into 1-inch pieces, then add them to the bowl with the pasta. Add the dressing and toss to combine.

Add the croutons and garnish with Parmesan cheese. Serve immediately or refrigerate, covered, until ready to serve.

Kelly's Note * *If you aren't serving the salad immediately, refrain from adding the croutons to avoid them getting soggy. To store the salad, cover it securely with plastic wrap and refrigerate it for up to 48 hours.*

Sweet and Sour Cucumber Salad

Secret ingredient

Honey-Roasted Peanuts

Cucumber salad makes an appearance across multiple cuisines, from *sunomono* in Japan to *gurkensalat* in Germany to *kachumber* in India. I even grew up eating my Hungarian grandmother's version of *uborkasalát*, which featured paper-thin cucumber slices soaked in a vinegary marinade, with plenty of sour cream and smoked paprika on top. Bottom line: Cucumbers are one heck of a worldly vegetable, and they need little more than a simple dressing to truly shine. I've opted for chunkier crescent shapes to bulk up your bowl, and looked to honey-roasted peanuts for a touch of sweet crunch.

PREP 15 minutes

COOK None

Yield *4 servings*

2 medium Persian or Japanese cucumbers

½ cup honey-roasted peanuts, chopped

½ cup rice vinegar

1 teaspoon sesame oil

1 teaspoon reduced-sodium soy sauce

2 teaspoons minced garlic

1 teaspoon sugar

Crushed red pepper flakes, for serving

Cut the cucumbers in half lengthwise and, using a spoon, scoop out the seeds. Slice the cucumbers into ¼-inch pieces, transfer to a bowl, and add the peanuts.

In a small bowl, whisk together the vinegar, sesame oil, soy sauce, garlic, and sugar. Add the dressing to the cucumbers and peanuts and toss to combine.

Top with crushed red pepper flakes to taste and serve.

Wedge Salad with Blue Cheese Dressing

Secret ingredient

Beets

There are two types of people in this world: those that love blue cheese and those that loathe it. The stinkier, the better, I say! I'll take it in dressing or dip form (see page 77), broiled atop a steak, or tucked into savory turnovers. I'll especially take it paired with sweet, earthy beets and crispy bacon, which all come together atop a chilled wedge of iceberg lettuce. There's no need to roast the beets prior to pureeing them, since your food processor will do all of the work to tenderize the root veggie. The result is a bright pink dressing that's guaranteed to leave your guests guessing about the surprise addition.

PREP	15 minutes
COOK	15 minutes
Yield	*4 servings*

FOR THE DRESSING

⅓ cup mayonnaise

⅓ cup sour cream

2 tablespoons buttermilk

1 tablespoon Worcestershire sauce

2 medium beets, peeled and roughly chopped

3 cloves garlic, roughly chopped

1 cup blue cheese crumbles, divided

Kosher salt and black pepper

FOR THE SALAD

8 slices bacon, cut into ½-inch pieces

2 cups halved cherry tomatoes

1 medium head iceberg lettuce, quartered

2 cups croutons

¼ cup chopped fresh chives

MAKE THE DRESSING In the bowl of a food processor, combine the mayonnaise, sour cream, buttermilk, Worcestershire, beets, and garlic and process until smooth. Add ½ cup of the blue cheese and process just until combined.

Stir in the remaining ½ cup blue cheese, then taste and season the dressing with salt and pepper.

MAKE THE SALAD Cook the bacon in a large skillet set over medium heat, draining the drippings into a heatproof bowl as needed, until all the fat has rendered. Using a slotted spoon, transfer the bacon to a paper towel–lined plate and reserve the bacon drippings.

Return enough of the set-aside bacon drippings to the skillet to make 2 tablespoons. Add the cherry tomatoes and cook over high heat, stirring, until blistered, about 3 minutes. Remove the tomatoes from the heat.

To assemble the salad, spoon about ¼ cup of the dressing down the center of each of four plates. Set a wedge of lettuce on each plate, then top with the remaining dressing. Scatter around the tomatoes, bacon pieces, croutons, and chives and serve.

Greek Chopped Salad

*Halloumi
Cheese*

No matter how you slice, shred, tear, or toss them, greens are always the most boring part of any salad. You can keep your lettuces, leaves, and weeds; I'll take all the good stuff—the chopped veggies, the salty olives, the hearty beans, and, most important, the warm cheese. That leads us here, to a lettuce-less, feta-less Greek salad that's anything *but* a boring side. In the spirit of making over this classic, I've retired the wilted romaine and introduced cubed halloumi, a sturdy Greek cheese that holds up well in a frying pan without melting into a mess.

PREP	20 minutes
COOK	10 minutes
Yield	*4 to 6 servings*

FOR THE SALAD

4 medium plum tomatoes, seeded and chopped

½ cup kalamata olives, pitted and halved

1 cup diced cucumber

1 cup diced green bell pepper

½ cup diced red onion

1 (15-ounce) can garbanzo beans (chickpeas), drained and rinsed

8 ounces halloumi cheese

2 tablespoons extra-virgin olive oil

FOR THE DRESSING

⅓ cup extra-virgin olive oil

¼ cup red wine vinegar

1½ teaspoons dried oregano

¼ teaspoon kosher salt

MAKE THE SALAD In a large bowl, stir together the tomatoes, olives, cucumber, bell pepper, red onion, and beans. Set aside.

Drain and dry the halloumi, then cut it into ½-inch cubes. Heat the olive oil in a skillet set over medium heat. Once the oil is hot, add the halloumi and cook, undisturbed, until golden brown on one side, about 5 minutes. Flip the cheese and continue browning on all sides, then using a slotted spoon, transfer the halloumi to the bowl with the salad.

MAKE THE DRESSING In a small bowl, whisk together the olive oil, vinegar, oregano, and salt.

Add the dressing to the salad, toss to combine, and serve.

Stone Fruit Salad

Summer months usher in all the good stuff on the fruit front, so when peaches and cherries hit their peak, I prefer to enjoy them fresh, unbaked, and outside the pie shell. They take the lead in this fruit-forward salad, where piquant red onions, creamy goat cheese, and salted pistachios get a little extra love from a jam-based dressing. If blueberry jam isn't readily available near you, any other variety—including grape, apricot, or marmalade—will pair just as well with the splash of Champagne vinegar and plenty of black pepper.

PREP	20 minutes
COOK	None
Yield	*4 servings*

4 cups mixed greens

2 medium peaches, pitted and sliced

1½ cups cherries, pitted and halved

¼ cup thinly sliced red onion

4 ounces goat cheese, crumbled

½ cup shelled roasted, salted pistachios

2 tablespoons blueberry jam

1½ tablespoons Champagne vinegar

1½ teaspoons minced shallot

½ teaspoon kosher salt

¼ teaspoon black pepper

¼ cup extra-virgin olive oil

In a large bowl, combine the mixed greens, peaches, cherries, red onion, goat cheese, and pistachios.

In a small bowl, whisk together the jam, vinegar, shallot, salt, and pepper. While whisking, stream in the olive oil and continue whisking until emulsified.

Pour the dressing over the salad, then toss to combine and serve.

Pastas

Mushroom Ravioli
(recipe, page 141)

30-Minute Macaroni and Cheese

Pumpkin

Canned pumpkin is a pantry staple year-round in our house. While it's most famous for its starring role in breakfast carbs (page 48) and snack cakes (page 246), I consider pumpkin to be widely underused—and underrated—on the savory front. It's impossible to detect when whisked into the creamy cheese sauce for my mac and cheese and intensifies the dish's classic color. But highest on this pro-pumpkin mom's list is the sneaky addition of vitamins, minerals, and antioxidants in every ooey-gooey, veggie-packed serving.

PREP	10 minutes
COOK	20 minutes
Yield	*6 servings*

1 pound uncooked medium shell pasta

2½ cups whole milk

1 (15-ounce) can pumpkin puree

½ cup (1 stick) unsalted butter

½ cup all-purpose flour

¼ teaspoon ground nutmeg

2 cups shredded Gruyère cheese

2 cups shredded sharp cheddar cheese

½ teaspoon kosher salt

¼ teaspoon black pepper

Bring a large pot of salted water to a boil. Add the pasta and cook until al dente, 10 to 12 minutes. Drain the pasta and set it aside.

While the pasta is cooking, in a medium saucepan set over medium heat, whisk together the milk and pumpkin puree. Warm the mixture until it is hot but not boiling, about 5 minutes. Remove the pot from the heat and set aside.

Heat the butter in a large heavy-bottomed stockpot set over medium heat. Once the butter has melted, whisk in the flour and cook, whisking constantly, until the mixture becomes light brown in color and has a slightly toasted aroma, about 3 minutes.

Whisk in the nutmeg, then remove the pot from the heat and slowly whisk in the pumpkin mixture. It will thicken, then thin out gradually and become smooth as you continue whisking.

Return the pot to medium heat and whisk in the Gruyère cheese, cheddar cheese, salt, and pepper. Cook until the cheese is melted, about 2 minutes.

Stir the pasta into the sauce until combined and serve.

Cacio e Pepe

Secret ingredient

Lemon

Cacio e pepe was one of the first dishes I ever mastered. It has become a dinnertime staple because it's quick, affordable, and easily topped with whatever protein I have on hand, from grilled chicken to fried eggs. Freshly grating the cheese is essential so that all it takes is a bit of hot pasta water to yield a silky-smooth sauce. Add some citrus to the mix and this lemony, peppery, adult version of buttered noodles will be on your table in 25 minutes or less.

PREP	10 minutes
COOK	15 minutes
Yield	*4 to 6 servings*

1 pound uncooked pasta, such as bucatini or spaghetti

3 tablespoons unsalted butter

1½ teaspoons coarsely ground black pepper

1 cup freshly grated Parmesan cheese

½ cup freshly grated Pecorino Romano cheese

1½ teaspoons grated lemon zest

1 tablespoon fresh lemon juice

Bring a large pot of salted water to a boil. Add the pasta and cook until al dente, 10 to 12 minutes, or according to package instructions. Reserve 1 cup of the pasta water, then drain the pasta and set it aside.

Heat the butter in a large saucepan set over medium heat. Once the butter has melted, add the black pepper and cook, stirring, for 2 minutes. Add ½ cup of the reserved pasta water and cook for 1 minute. Remove the pan from the heat and quickly whisk in the Parmesan and Pecorino one third at a time, then whisk in the lemon zest and lemon juice.

Add half of the pasta to the saucepan and toss to combine with the sauce, then add the remaining pasta and continue tossing until it is well coated. If the sauce becomes too thick at any point, stir in the remaining pasta water, 2 tablespoons at a time, until it reaches your desired consistency. Serve immediately.

Sweet and Spicy Penne Arrabbiata

Secret ingredient

Strawberries

I am an admitted wimp when it comes to spicy foods. While some people crave heat, I can be found fishing the jalapeños out of guacamole. (I know, I know.) So when it comes to pasta, fiery arrabbiata sauce has never been high on my list . . . that is, until I added strawberries to the mix. The natural sugars in the fruit marry with the spice of crushed red pepper flakes, leading to the perfect amount of sweet heat. This sauce is definitely worth the longer simmer time, which gives the flavors a chance to really mingle while it reduces, thickens, and becomes jammy in consistency.

PREP	15 minutes
COOK	1 hour 50 minutes
Yield	*4 to 6 servings*

3 tablespoons extra-virgin olive oil

½ cup minced yellow onion

½ teaspoon crushed red pepper flakes, plus more to taste

4 large cloves garlic, minced

1 (28-ounce) can diced tomatoes, preferably San Marzano

3 cups diced strawberries

1 tablespoon tomato paste

2 teaspoons dried basil

½ teaspoon kosher salt, plus more for seasoning

¼ teaspoon black pepper, plus more for seasoning

1 pound uncooked penne pasta

Heat the olive oil in a large skillet set over medium heat. Once the oil is hot, add the onion and crushed red pepper flakes and cook, stirring, until the onion is translucent, about 5 minutes. Add the garlic and continue cooking, stirring, for an additional 2 minutes.

Stir in the tomatoes, strawberries, tomato paste, basil, salt, and pepper. Simmer the sauce, stirring occasionally, until it thickens and becomes jammy in consistency, about 30 minutes, while you cook the pasta.

Bring a large pot of salted water to a boil. Add the pasta and cook until al dente, 10 to 12 minutes. Drain.

Taste and season the sauce with additional salt and pepper. In a large bowl, toss together the pasta and sauce and serve.

Stuffed Shells with No-Mato Sauce

Tomatoes need not apply for this creamy, flavor-packed pasta that's an updated take on good ol' stuffed shells. Jarred roasted red peppers take the lead, imparting both subtly sweet flavor and bold color to the tomato-free sauce. I've kept the filling classic—a mixture of sweet or spicy Italian sausage, ricotta cheese, and Italian spices—but for those looking to go the vegetarian route, you could easily sub in a 10-ounce package of frozen (drained and thawed) spinach for the sausage.

PREP	25 minutes
COOK	50 minutes
Yield	*6 servings*

FOR THE NO-MATO SAUCE

3 tablespoons extra-virgin olive oil

2 medium carrots, peeled and diced

1 yellow onion, diced

1 tablespoon minced garlic

2 (16-ounce) jars roasted red peppers, drained

⅓ cup loosely packed fresh basil leaves, plus more for garnish (optional)

2 tablespoons red wine vinegar

1 tablespoon sugar

1 teaspoon kosher salt

½ teaspoon black pepper

FOR THE PASTA SHELLS

24 uncooked jumbo pasta shells (about 7 ounces)

1 pound sweet or spicy Italian sausage, casings removed

1 cup whole-milk ricotta cheese

1 large egg

1½ teaspoons dried oregano

1½ cups shredded mozzarella cheese

MAKE THE SAUCE Heat the oil in a large skillet set over medium heat. Once the oil is hot, add the carrots and onion and cook, stirring, until the carrots are fork-tender, about 12 minutes. Add the garlic and cook, stirring, until golden, about 2 minutes.

Transfer the ingredients to a blender, add the roasted red peppers, basil, vinegar, sugar, salt, and pepper, and blend until pureed. Taste and season the sauce with salt and pepper.

Pour half of the sauce into the bottom of a 13x9-inch baking pan. Set the remaining sauce aside.

COOK AND STUFF THE SHELLS Preheat the oven to 350°F.

Bring a large pot of salted water to a boil. Add the pasta shells and cook until al dente, about 9 minutes. Drain, rinse with cool water, and set aside.

Meanwhile, cook the sausage in a large nonstick skillet over medium heat, breaking it apart with a spatula, until no longer pink. Using a slotted spoon, transfer the sausage to a bowl and let cool completely.

continued

Once the sausage has cooled, stir in the ricotta cheese, egg, and oregano. Divide the sausage mixture among the shells, using a spoon to stuff each. Arrange the stuffed shells in a single layer in the baking dish and top with the remaining sauce.

Bake the shells for 20 minutes.

Remove the baking dish from the oven. Carefully position an oven rack about 4 inches from the broiler and preheat the broiler. Sprinkle the mozzarella cheese on top of the shells. Return the baking dish to the oven and broil until the cheese is melted and begins to brown slightly, about 2 minutes.

Garnish with additional basil, if desired, and serve.

Broccoli Pesto Pasta

Green Olives

Pesto is one food that everyone in my house can agree on. Even my toddler boys gobble up this pesto pasta by the bowlful because there's not a trace of broccoli flavor in sight. Hidden veggies for the mom-win! I attribute the green color of this creamy pasta to the olives—one of their favorite foods—so mealtime is protest-free. The brininess of the olives seasons the sauce with its natural saltiness, while basil works its fresh herb magic. Best of all, this pasta can be served warm, room temp, or chilled, making it a go-to dish year-round.

PREP	20 minutes
COOK	13 minutes
Yield	*4 to 6 servings*

2 cups broccoli florets

1 pound uncooked pasta, such as rigatoni or penne

3 tablespoons pine nuts

1 cup green olives, pitted

2 cups fresh basil leaves

3 cloves garlic, roughly chopped

3 tablespoons freshly grated Parmesan cheese

¼ teaspoon black pepper, plus more for seasoning

¼ cup extra-virgin olive oil

Kosher salt, for seasoning

Bring a large pot of salted water to a boil. Add the broccoli florets and cook for 1 minute. Using a slotted spoon, transfer the broccoli to a blender.

Bring the water back to a boil. Add the pasta and cook until al dente, 10 to 12 minutes, or according to package instructions. Drain the pasta, reserving 1 cup of the pasta water.

Cook the pine nuts in a small saucepan set over medium heat, moving the nuts around, until fragrant and toasted, about 3 minutes.

Add the pine nuts to the broccoli in the blender, along with the olives, basil, garlic, Parmesan cheese, pepper, and ½ cup of the reserved pasta water. Pulse until combined.

With the blender running, stream in the olive oil, stopping the blender and scraping down the sides as needed, until the pesto is pureed. Taste and season with salt and additional pepper.

In a large bowl, toss together the pasta with your desired amount of pesto, thinning it with additional reserved pasta water 2 tablespoons at a time as needed. Serve.

Kelly's Note * *Leftover pesto? Pour it into ice cube trays, then cover securely with plastic wrap and freeze. When ready to serve, pop out a pesto cube or two and defrost in the microwave or on the stovetop with your pasta of choice.*

Simple Skillet
Lasagna (recipe,
page 132)

Simple Skillet Lasagna

Secret ingredient

Refrigerated Ravioli

I am all for the labor of love that is homemade lasagna, but when the cheesy pasta craving strikes, I need satisfaction, stat. I've trimmed the prep time down to a speedy 15 minutes by utilizing one of the grocery store's most underrated shortcuts: refrigerated ravioli. You still achieve the classic flavor of lasagna, but without all the mess and stress of layering noodles and fillings. A quick-fix meat sauce lends this dish that homemade touch, but if you're really in a pinch, jarred sauce gets this mom's stamp of approval. (*Pictured on the preceding pages, 130–131.*)

PREP	15 minutes
COOK	35 minutes
Yield	*6 servings*

1 (20-ounce) package refrigerated ravioli of any type

1 pound sweet or spicy Italian sausage, casings removed

1 tablespoon minced garlic

1 (28-ounce) can crushed tomatoes

1 (15-ounce) can tomato sauce

2 tablespoons minced fresh oregano

1 tablespoon sugar

½ teaspoon kosher salt, plus more for seasoning

¼ teaspoon black pepper, plus more for seasoning

8 ounces shredded mozzarella cheese, divided

Position an oven rack about 4 inches from the broiler and preheat the oven to 375°F.

Bring a large pot of salted water to a boil. Add the ravioli and cook according to the package directions just until al dente. Drain the ravioli and set aside.

In a large cast-iron skillet or sauté pan set over medium-high heat, cook the sausage, breaking it apart with a spatula, until cooked through and no longer pink. Add the garlic and cook, stirring, for 2 minutes. Add the crushed tomatoes, tomato sauce, oregano, sugar, salt, and pepper. Cook for 5 minutes, then taste and season the sauce with additional salt and pepper.

Add the ravioli to the skillet and toss to combine. Stir in half of the shredded mozzarella cheese, then sprinkle the remaining mozzarella cheese on top. Bake for 10 minutes. Turn on the broiler, transfer the skillet to the oven rack directly under the broiler, and broil until the cheese begins to bubble and brown, about 2 minutes.

Remove the skillet from the oven and serve.

Shrimp Scampi Linguine

Croutons are to salad what breadcrumbs are to shrimp scampi: You don't really notice them when they're there, but you definitely miss them when they're gone. They provide a welcome textural crunch that's even more essential once pasta joins the shrimp scampi party. So, rather than serve the pasta with a side of bread for dipping, I've taken your stale loaf and turned it into crispy, lemony breadcrumbs that are perfect for soaking up all that garlicky sauce. I am all for marinara-free sauces, and the combination here of garlic, white wine, lemon juice, and fresh parsley is a tried-and-tested winner.

PREP	30 minutes
COOK	35 minutes
Yield	*4 servings*

FOR THE LEMONY BREADCRUMBS

2 cups roughly torn crusty bread, such as ciabatta or sourdough

1½ teaspoons grated lemon zest

2 tablespoons unsalted butter

½ teaspoon kosher salt

FOR THE PASTA

12 ounces uncooked linguine

4 tablespoons unsalted butter, divided

1 tablespoon minced garlic

¼ teaspoon crushed red pepper flakes (optional)

1 pound medium shrimp, shelled and deveined, tails removed

Kosher salt and black pepper

½ cup dry white wine

¼ cup fresh lemon juice

2 tablespoons extra-virgin olive oil

⅓ cup chopped fresh Italian parsley

MAKE THE BREADCRUMBS Preheat the oven to 350°F.

Spread the bread in an even layer on a baking sheet and bake until dried out and crispy, about 10 minutes. Combine the bread and lemon zest in the bowl of a food processor and pulse until the bread is coarsely ground.

Heat the butter in a large skillet set over medium heat. Once the butter is hot, add the breadcrumbs and cook, stirring, until they are golden brown and crisp, about 5 minutes. Stir in the salt, then transfer the breadcrumbs to a bowl. Wipe out the pan.

MAKE THE PASTA Bring a large pot of salted water to a boil. Add the linguine and cook until al dente, 10 to 12 minutes. While the pasta cooks, make the sauce.

In the large skillet set over medium-low heat, heat 2 tablespoons of the butter. Once the butter has melted, add the garlic and crushed red pepper flakes (if using) and cook, stirring, until the garlic is golden brown, about 2 minutes. Add the shrimp and cook, turning as needed, until pink and cooked through, about 3 minutes. Using a slotted spoon, transfer the shrimp to a bowl. Season with salt and pepper.

Increase the heat to medium, then add the wine and lemon juice to the skillet, scraping up any brown bits. Cook until the liquid has reduced by half. Add the remaining 2 tablespoons butter and the olive oil and simmer for 2 minutes.

Drain the pasta and add it to the pan along with the shrimp and parsley. Toss to combine. Garnish with the breadcrumbs and serve.

Gnocchi alla Vodka

Give my dad, Drew, an Italian restaurant menu, and ten times out of ten, he'll order the gnocchi. He is a potato dumpling connoisseur who will pair any sauce with gnocchi, as long as they are pillowy, fluffy, and topped with plenty of Parmesan. But homemade gnocchi tend to get a bad rap. They require a multistep process, extreme patience, and the acceptance that even after *all that work*, you may still end up with chewy, dense dumplings. Failure is no longer an option, thanks to your new secret weapon: baking powder. The leavener lightens, fluffs, and foolproofs the dough, yielding soft, airy gnocchi. A quick-fix vodka sauce, complete with crunchy bacon bites, makes this recipe 100-percent Drew-Approved. (*Pictured on the following pages, 136–137.*)

PREP	45 minutes
COOK	50 minutes
Yield	*4 to 6 servings*

FOR THE GNOCCHI

2 pounds russet potatoes (about 3 medium potatoes)

1 cup all-purpose flour, plus more for dusting working surface

1 large egg

1½ teaspoons kosher salt

1 teaspoon baking powder

FOR THE VODKA SAUCE

6 slices bacon, diced

3 cloves garlic, minced

½ cup vodka

1 (28-ounce) can crushed tomatoes

½ cup heavy cream

1½ tablespoons sugar

1 teaspoon kosher salt

½ teaspoon black pepper

———

Freshly grated Parmesan cheese, for serving

MAKE THE GNOCCHI In a large stockpot, cover the potatoes with cold water and bring to a boil. Boil until the potatoes are fork-tender, about 45 minutes. Remove the potatoes from the water and let cool until you can safely handle them.

Using a paring knife or peeler, remove the skins, then cut the potatoes into quarters.

Lightly flour a baking sheet. Pass the potatoes through a ricer directly onto the baking sheet and let cool completely.

Lightly flour your work surface. Add the cooled potatoes, gathering them into a mound with a well in the center. Add the egg and salt to the well, then lightly whisk the egg.

Using your hands, slowly knead together the potato and egg, then add ½ cup flour and the baking powder, kneading until the dough begins to come together. Add the remaining ½ cup flour and knead just until smooth. (The longer you knead the dough, the more gluten will form and the tougher your gnocchi will be, so keep the kneading to a minimum.)

Cut the dough into six equal pieces.

Clean and lightly flour your work surface. Roll each piece of dough into a ½-inch-thick rope. Cut each rope into ½-inch pieces to form the gnocchi. Gently press each gnocchi across the back of a fork to form the indentations.

Bring a large pot of salted water to a boil. Add the gnocchi in batches and cook until they float to the top, about 1 minute. Using a slotted spoon, transfer the gnocchi to a bowl and set them aside while you make the sauce.

MAKE THE SAUCE Cook the bacon in a large sauté pan set over medium heat, stirring, until all of the fat has rendered. Using a slotted spoon, transfer the bacon to a plate and leave 3 tablespoons of drippings in the pan.

Add the garlic to the bacon drippings and cook, stirring, until golden brown, about 2 minutes. Add the vodka and cook until it has mostly evaporated, about 3 minutes. Add the crushed tomatoes, then whisk in the cream, sugar, salt, and pepper. Cook the sauce, stirring occasionally, until it is warmed through. Stir two-thirds of the cooked bacon into the sauce.

In a large bowl, toss the gnocchi with the sauce, then transfer to plates. Garnish with Parmesan cheese and the remaining bacon and serve.

Gnocchi alla Vodka
(recipe, page 134)

Orecchiette with Greens and Beans

Secret ingredient

Rainbow Chard

Quick! Name a leafy green. If you're like most people, kale and spinach are first to come to mind. They tend to have a monopoly on the trendy greens market, with the less-popular chard standing on the sidelines just begging to be put into the game. It's time for chard to shine in all its rainbow glory, and it's ready to do so alongside its biggest cheerleaders, bacon and white beans. The garlicky sauce is made with seasoned pasta water, fresh lemon juice, and ample Parmesan for an eight-ingredient dish that packs big flavor on a little budget.

PREP	15 minutes
COOK	35 minutes
Yield	*6 to 8 servings*

1 pound uncooked orecchiette pasta

8 slices bacon, cut into ½-inch pieces

2 tablespoons extra-virgin olive oil

3 cloves garlic, thinly sliced

1 (15.5-ounce) can cannellini beans, rinsed and drained

¼ cup fresh lemon juice

1 pound rainbow chard, stemmed and roughly chopped

¾ cup freshly grated Parmesan cheese, divided

Bring a large pot of salted water to a boil. Add the pasta and cook until al dente, 10 to 12 minutes. Reserve 1 cup of the pasta water, then drain the pasta and set aside.

Cook the bacon in a heavy-bottomed stockpot set over medium heat until all the fat has rendered and the bacon is crisp. Using a slotted spoon, transfer the bacon to a plate, then remove all but 2 tablespoons of drippings from the pot.

Add the olive oil to the pot, then add the garlic and cook, stirring, until slightly crispy and golden brown, about 3 minutes. Stir in the cannellini beans, then add the lemon juice and cook, stirring, for 2 minutes. Add ½ cup of the reserved pasta water and the chard and cook until the liquid is absorbed and the chard is wilted. Stir in the remaining ½ cup pasta water and ½ cup of the Parmesan cheese and cook, stirring, until the liquid is absorbed.

Stir in the pasta and reserved bacon. Garnish the pasta with the remaining Parmesan cheese and serve.

Spaghetti and Turkey Meatballs

Everyone has their spin on this classic—mine comes in the form of a toasty spice. Turkey meatballs are on the regular rotation at our house, and this recipe (without the cinnamon) gets combined with a whole range of sauces, from marinara and barbecue to teriyaki and sweet chili. It's hard to imagine the addition of a single spice really transforming something as ordinary as meatballs, but the warmth and earthy flavor of cinnamon boldly shines through. In fact, the meatballs themselves are *so* flavorful, we often enjoy them sans any sauce at all. To do so, simply cook the meatballs all the way through during the browning stage, then skewer and devour!

PREP	25 minutes
COOK	30 minutes
Yield	*4 to 6 servings*

FOR THE MEATBALLS

2 tablespoons whole milk

1 slice white bread, roughly torn

1 pound ground turkey

½ cup freshly grated Parmesan cheese

1 large egg, lightly beaten

2 teaspoons minced garlic

2 teaspoons dried basil

1½ teaspoons ground cinnamon

½ teaspoon kosher salt

¼ teaspoon black pepper

2 tablespoons extra-virgin olive oil, plus more if needed

FOR THE SAUCE

1 tablespoon minced garlic

½ cup dry white wine

1 (28-ounce) can crushed tomatoes

1½ tablespoons sugar

1 teaspoon kosher salt

½ teaspoon pepper

1 pound uncooked spaghetti

———

Freshly grated Parmesan cheese, for serving

MAKE THE MEATBALLS In a small bowl, drizzle the milk over the bread and stir to combine. Let the mixture sit for 5 minutes, then mash it together with a fork.

In a large bowl, combine the bread mixture, turkey, Parmesan cheese, egg, garlic, basil, cinnamon, salt, and pepper. Using your hands, mix until just combined. Scoop out 1½-tablespoon portions of the mixture and roll into balls.

Heat the olive oil in a large sauté pan or Dutch oven set over medium heat. Add the meatballs in batches and cook until browned (do not cook them all the way through), adding more oil as needed. Transfer the meatballs to a plate, leaving in the pot all the brown bits and drippings for the sauce.

MAKE THE SAUCE Reduce the heat to medium-low. If needed, supplement the drippings in the pot with enough olive oil to lightly coat the entire bottom of the pot. Add the garlic and cook, stirring, until golden brown and fragrant, about 2 minutes. Add the wine and cook, scraping up the brown bits, until the liquid has almost completely evaporated, about 3 minutes.

continued

Stir in the crushed tomatoes, sugar, salt, and pepper. Return the browned meatballs to the pot and simmer in the sauce until they are cooked through, about 15 minutes.

While the meatballs are simmering, bring a large pot of salted water to a boil. Add the spaghetti and cook until al dente, 10 to 12 minutes. Drain the spaghetti.

When ready to serve, top the spaghetti with the meatballs and sauce. Garnish with Parmesan cheese and serve.

Mushroom Ravioli with Brown Butter Sauce

If you're up for the ultimate pasta project, then allow me to introduce you to the single greatest homemade ravioli you'll ever taste. That's a bold claim, but when mushrooms, shallots, thyme, and wine find a friend in tangy goat cheese, there's just no topping this filling. I'll be totally honest: This is not a weeknight endeavor. This is a labor of love and a special occasion meal that's worth every single minute of effort. The good news is the ravioli freeze like a breeze, so you can whip up a batch or two, then store the extras for when you're in need of a faster DIY pasta fix.

PREP	2 hours
COOK	25 minutes
Yield	*6 servings*

2 cups all-purpose flour, plus more if needed

3 large eggs, lightly whisked

1½ teaspoons kosher salt, divided

2 tablespoons extra-virgin olive oil

¼ cup minced shallots

2 cloves garlic, minced

3 cups cremini mushrooms, stemmed and quartered

½ cup dry white wine

2 tablespoons chopped fresh thyme, divided

¼ teaspoon black pepper

4 ounces goat cheese, at room temperature

½ cup (1 stick) unsalted butter

Freshly grated Parmesan cheese, for serving

● **EQUIPMENT**
Pasta roller or stand mixer attachment

Mound the flour on your work surface and create a well in the center. Add the eggs and 1 teaspoon of the salt into the center of the well. Using a fork, slowly work the flour into the eggs until the dough starts to come together.

Using your hands, work the remaining flour into the dough, adding additional flour as needed if the dough is too wet. Knead the dough for 3 minutes, then cover with plastic wrap and let rest at room temperature for 30 minutes while you make the ravioli filling.

Heat the olive oil in a large skillet set over medium heat. Add the shallots and garlic and cook, stirring, until the garlic is golden, about 2 minutes. Add the mushrooms, wine, 1 tablespoon of the thyme, remaining ½ teaspoon salt, and the pepper and cook, stirring, until the liquid has almost completely evaporated and the mushrooms are tender, about 10 minutes. Remove from the heat and set aside to cool completely.

continued

Once the mixture is cool, transfer to the bowl of a food processor, add the goat cheese, and blend until the mixture is smooth. Transfer the filling to a sealable plastic bag and snip off a corner, or into a piping bag.

Divide the dough into six equal portions and cover with a dish towel or plastic wrap. Lightly flour a baking sheet and set aside.

Pass one portion of the dough through the pasta machine, then lightly flour it and change the settings so that the rollers are closer together. Pass the pasta through the machine again several times, moving the rollers closer together after each pass, until the pasta is paper-thin. Place the sheet of dough on the baking sheet and cover with a dish towel. Repeat the rolling process with the remaining pieces of dough, putting them side by side in a single layer on the baking sheet.

When you're ready to assemble the ravioli, bring a large pot of salted water to a boil.

Fill a small bowl with water. Lightly flour your work surface, then lay out one sheet of pasta dough. Pipe 1-tablespoon mounds of the filling into the lower half of the sheet, spacing each mound 3 inches apart. Wet your finger in the water, then run it around the long side of the sheet of dough and in between each mound of filling. Fold the sheet of pasta over the filling, carefully pressing out the air and sealing the filling in the dough. Using a ravioli cutter or cookie cutter, cut out your preferred ravioli shape. Repeat the filling and cutting process with the remaining filling and sheets of dough. (See Kelly's Notes.)

Melt the butter in a medium skillet set over medium heat and cook until it begins to turn golden brown in color and has a slightly nutty aroma, about 3 minutes. Stir in the remaining 1 tablespoon thyme. Remove the brown butter from the heat and set aside.

Add the ravioli in batches to the boiling water and boil until the pasta is cooked through, about 4 minutes. Using a slotted spoon, transfer the ravioli to a large bowl. Drizzle with the brown butter, sprinkle with Parmesan cheese, and serve.

Kelly's Notes * *Any shape or size works when making ravioli, as well as any method for folding and sealing the dough. A ravioli cutter or cookie cutter yields the cleanest results, but a sharp knife will also do the trick.*

Store uncooked ravioli in a single layer on a baking sheet covered securely with plastic wrap, or in a sealable plastic bag. To cook ravioli from the frozen state, bring a large pot of salted water to a boil, then add the ravioli straight from the freezer and cook until al dente. The cook time for frozen ravioli will be slightly longer than for fresh.

Fettuccine Alfredo with Lobster

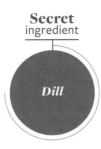

Fettuccine Alfredo is at the top of my list when it comes to casual comfort food. It's the complete indulgent trifecta of pasta, butter, and cheese. But what if you could pass off this kids' menu dish at an adult dinner party? Cue the lobster, tomatoes, corn, and dill! This is my elegant spin on the classic, featuring garlicky veggies, al dente fettuccini, and tender lobster tossed in a cheesy white wine sauce that's loaded with fresh dill. Take your presentation up a notch with halved lobster tails perched atop twirled towers of creamy carbs.

PREP	20 minutes
COOK	30 minutes
Yield	*4 to 6 servings*

4 medium lobster tails

2 tablespoons plus ½ cup unsalted butter

2 cups fresh or thawed frozen corn kernels

2 cups cherry tomatoes

1 tablespoon minced garlic

1 pound uncooked fettuccini

½ cup dry white wine

1 cup heavy cream

1 cup freshly grated Parmesan cheese

½ teaspoon kosher salt

¼ teaspoon black pepper

½ cup chopped fresh dill, plus more for serving

Bring a large pot of salted water to a boil. Using kitchen shears, cut lengthwise along the bottom side of the lobster tails. Boil the tails until opaque, about 5 minutes. Remove them from the water and set aside to cool. Set the pot aside and do not discard the water.

In a large sauté pan set over medium-high heat, combine 2 tablespoons butter, corn, and tomatoes. Cook, stirring, until the corn is tender and the tomatoes have softened, about 10 minutes. Add the garlic and cook, stirring, until fragrant, about 2 minutes.

Bring the pot of water back to a boil and add the fettuccini. Cook until al dente, 10 to 12 minutes.

While the pasta cooks, finish the sauce. Add the remaining ½ cup butter to the pan with the corn and tomatoes and cook until melted and bubbling. Add the wine and cook until the liquid has reduced by half, about 5 minutes. Add the cream and simmer until thickened, about 5 minutes. Add the Parmesan cheese, salt, and pepper and cook, stirring, until the cheese is melted, then add the dill.

Drain the pasta, add to the pan with the sauce, and toss to coat.

Remove the lobster tails from the shells. Chop two of the lobster tails into bite-size pieces, then split the remaining two tails in half lengthwise. Add the chopped lobster to the pasta and toss to combine.

Divide the pasta among serving plates and top each with a half lobster tail. Garnish with fresh dill and serve.

Entrées

Chicken Pot Pie
with Cheesy Drop
Biscuits (recipe,
page 163)

Crisped and
Dipped Chicken
Thighs (recipe,
page 152)

Crisped and Dipped Chicken Thighs

Secret
ingredient

Orange Marmalade

What do you get when a Southern staple like dipped fried chicken and a take-out favorite like orange chicken join forces? The best of both poultry worlds: extra-crispy skin and a sticky, citrusy glaze. I've ditched the deep-fryer and served up a simplified spin by searing and then baking the chicken thighs to ensure every bite is both crunchy and juicy. While dipped fried chicken is traditionally coated in a spicy, vinegary sauce, I've added a generous dollop of orange marmalade to shift this sauce toward the sweeter side so the whole family can get in on the action. (*Pictured on the preceding pages, 150–151.*)

PREP	15 minutes
COOK	40 minutes
Yield	*4 servings*

8 bone-in, skin-on chicken thighs

Kosher salt and black pepper, for seasoning

2 tablespoons vegetable oil

¼ cup hot sauce, such as Tabasco

¼ cup orange marmalade

2 tablespoons Worcestershire sauce

2 tablespoons rice vinegar

2 tablespoons unsalted butter, cold

Preheat the oven to 400°F. Line a rimmed baking sheet with foil and place a wire rack on top. Season the chicken thighs on both sides with salt and pepper.

Heat the oil in a large cast-iron skillet set over medium-high heat. Once the oil is hot, arrange half of the chicken thighs skin side down and cook them undisturbed until they are golden brown and release naturally from the pan, about 6 minutes. Flip the chicken thighs once and continue cooking for an additional 2 minutes. Transfer the thighs to the wire rack, then repeat the browning process with the second half of the chicken thighs.

Bake the chicken thighs for about 20 minutes, until they reach an internal temperature of 165°F.

While the chicken thighs are baking, in a small saucepan set over medium-low heat, whisk together the hot sauce, marmalade, Worcestershire, and vinegar. Cook the sauce, stirring occasionally, for 5 minutes, then stir in the butter and cook until the butter is melted and the sauce is warmed through.

Remove the chicken thighs from the oven. Spoon the sauce on top and serve immediately.

Chicken Cutlets with Apple Salad

My dad was born in Budapest, Hungary, so Eastern European Wiener schnitzel was on the regular rotation growing up. My mom mastered the art of the thinly pounded, breaded, and pan-fried cutlets, which we ended up calling "Little Guys" for a still-unknown reason. Nomenclature aside, Little Guys is one of the many family recipes I've continued cooking over the decades. I often switch up the crispy coating, swapping in everything from Japanese panko to crushed cheese crackers, which leads us to the trusty graham cracker, in breadcrumb form. The toasty sweetness of the grahams pairs perfectly with tart apples and peppery arugula for a go-to meal that's easy enough for weeknight family dinners but sophisticated enough for weekend dinner parties.

PREP	20 minutes
COOK	20 minutes
Yield	*4 servings*

FOR THE CHICKEN

4 medium boneless, skinless chicken breasts

Kosher salt and black pepper, for seasoning

9 sheets graham crackers

1 cup panko breadcrumbs

⅔ cup all-purpose flour

2 large eggs

¼ cup milk

Unsalted butter, for sautéing

Extra-virgin olive oil, for sautéing

FOR THE SALAD

¼ cup extra-virgin olive oil

1 teaspoon grated lemon zest

¼ cup fresh lemon juice

2 teaspoons honey

2 teaspoons minced garlic

½ teaspoon kosher salt

¼ teaspoon black pepper

3 cups arugula

1 large Granny Smith apple, cored and cut into matchsticks

⅓ cup thinly sliced red onion

MAKE THE CHICKEN Place one chicken breast in a sealable plastic bag. Press out the air and seal it closed. Using a meat mallet or a heavy skillet, pound the chicken breast until it is ½ inch thick all around. Repeat with the remaining chicken breasts, season them with salt and pepper, then set aside.

Add the graham crackers to the bowl of a food processor and blend until finely ground. Transfer to a shallow bowl and stir in the breadcrumbs. Add the flour to a second shallow bowl. Whisk together the eggs and milk in a third shallow bowl.

Dredge the chicken cutlets in the flour, shaking off any excess, then dip them in the egg mixture. Dredge the chicken cutlets in the graham cracker mixture, pressing to coat the chicken all over.

Heat 1 tablespoon butter and 2 tablespoons olive oil in a large skillet set over medium heat. Once the butter has melted and the mixture is hot, add one or two cutlets to the pan. Cook, undisturbed, until golden brown, about 5 minutes, then flip the cutlets once and continue cooking until cooked

continued

Chicken Cutlets
with Apple Salad,
continued

through, about 3 minutes longer. Transfer the cutlets to plates and season with salt. Wipe out the skillet, then repeat the cooking process with the remaining cutlets.

MAKE THE SALAD In a large bowl, whisk together the olive oil, lemon zest, lemon juice, honey, garlic, salt, and pepper. Add the arugula, apple, and red onion and toss to combine.

Top the chicken cutlets with the arugula salad and serve.

Kelly's Note ∗ *The cutlets can be breaded up to a day in advance and stored, covered, in the refrigerator until ready to cook.*

Tex-Mex Turkey Burgers with Chipotle Mayo

Secret ingredient

Creamed Corn

Ground turkey has it rough in the reputation department. It's notoriously dry and flavorless, especially in burger form, and it's usually only preferred to beef when healthiness is a factor. But not for long! We can finally take back the bad rap of crumbly turkey burgers everywhere with these moist and juicy Tex-Mex-inspired patties, all thanks to a humble can of creamed corn. On the flavor front, we've got spices, herbs, veggies, cheese, *and* a chipotle mayo, so there's no chance this formerly blank canvas is going to be a bland burger.

PREP	15 minutes
COOK	15 minutes
Yield	*4 servings*

FOR THE MAYO

½ cup mayonnaise

2 teaspoons sauce from canned chipotles in adobo sauce

2 teaspoons fresh lime juice

½ teaspoon kosher salt

FOR THE BURGERS

1 pound lean ground turkey

¼ cup canned creamed corn

¼ cup breadcrumbs

1 large egg

¼ cup minced onion

2 tablespoons chopped fresh cilantro

1½ teaspoons ground cumin

½ teaspoon kosher salt

½ teaspoon black pepper

Cooking spray

4 slices Monterey Jack cheese

4 brioche hamburger buns

Lettuce, tomato, and avocado, for topping

MAKE THE MAYO In a large bowl, whisk together the mayonnaise, adobo sauce, lime juice, and salt. Cover and refrigerate for up to 2 days.

MAKE THE BURGERS In a large bowl, combine the ground turkey, creamed corn, breadcrumbs, egg, onion, cilantro, cumin, salt, and pepper. Using your hands, mix together the ingredients just until combined. Shape the mixture into four patties.

Heat a large skillet over medium heat, then coat the skillet with cooking spray. Add the patties and cook for 5 minutes on one side, then flip them and cook until they are no longer pink and have reached an internal temperature of 165°F, an additional 10 minutes. Top each burger with a slice of cheese.

Spread a portion of the chipotle mayo on the bottom half of each bun. Top the mayo with a burger, then add lettuce, tomato, avocado, and the top half of the bun and serve.

Kelly's Note ✳ *Leftover creamed corn can be sealed in a plastic bag or airtight container and frozen for up to 1 month.*

Sticky Pineapple Chicken

There's just something about a meal served in a pineapple bowl that transports me somewhere beyond my kitchen table. Hawaii, Bora Bora, Fiji: You name the tropical destination, and Sticky Pineapple Chicken will take your taste buds there. I originally shared a variation of this recipe on Just a Taste in 2017, and it quickly racked up more than 100 five-star reviews. I attribute the high praise to a combination of the prep time (a speedy 30 minutes) and the incredible flavor of tender chicken thighs and crunchy macadamia nuts tossed in the perfect sweet, tangy, garlicky sauce. It's a guaranteed dinner winner!

PREP	15 minutes
COOK	15 minutes
Yield	*4 servings*

½ cup pineapple juice

⅓ cup soy sauce

⅓ cup chicken broth

⅓ cup hoisin sauce

½ cup packed brown sugar

1 tablespoon minced garlic

2 teaspoons cornstarch

1 tablespoon extra-virgin olive oil

1½ pounds boneless, skinless chicken thighs, cut into 1-inch cubes

Kosher salt and black pepper, for seasoning

1 cup diced canned or fresh pineapple

1 cup macadamia nuts, roughly chopped

Coconut rice (page 188), for serving

In a medium saucepan, whisk together the pineapple juice, soy sauce, broth, hoisin sauce, brown sugar, garlic, and cornstarch. Bring the mixture to a boil over medium heat and cook until the sauce has reduced to about 1 cup and is the consistency of a thick syrup, about 5 minutes. Set the sauce aside.

Heat the olive oil in a large nonstick skillet set over medium-high heat. Once the oil is hot, add the chicken and season with salt and pepper. Cook the chicken, stirring, until it is no longer pink, 7 to 10 minutes.

Drain any liquid from the skillet, then add the sauce and stir until combined. Add the pineapple and macadamia nuts and cook, stirring, for an additional 1 minute.

Divide the rice among serving plates or hollowed-out halved pineapples, then spoon the chicken mixture on top and serve.

Healthy White Chicken Chili

Secret ingredient

Hummus

Hummus? In chili? Yes indeed! You may be scratching your head on this one, but a single spoonful of this creamy yet cream-less chicken chili will make you a believer. There's not one, but *two* entire containers of garlic hummus in the chili. It makes itself known both in flavor and texture, and the result is an ultra-healthy, super-hearty meal-in-a-bowl that's easily adaptable to any diet. Vegetarian? Swap in vegetable broth and ditch the chicken. Vegan? Take it a step further and skip the cheese topping.

PREP	20 minutes
COOK	20 minutes
Yield	*6 to 8 servings*

1 tablespoon extra-virgin olive oil

1 small yellow onion, diced

1 (7-ounce) can diced green chiles

2 teaspoons ground cumin

¼ teaspoon chili powder

4 cups chicken broth

2 (17-ounce) containers garlic hummus

3 tablespoons fresh lime juice

1 rotisserie chicken, skin and bones removed and meat shredded

2 (15-ounce) cans cannellini beans, rinsed and drained

Shredded cheddar cheese, for serving

Diced avocado, for serving

Sliced scallions, for serving

Heat the olive oil in a large stockpot set over medium-low heat. Once the oil is warm, add the onion and cook, stirring, until translucent, about 8 minutes. Add the chiles, cumin, and chili powder and cook, stirring, for 2 minutes. Whisk in the broth, hummus, and lime juice, mixing until combined. Stir in the chicken and beans and cook until warmed through, 5 to 7 minutes.

Serve the chili topped with cheese, avocado, and scallions.

Chicken Tikka Masala Meatballs

Cinnamon Applesauce

Indian cuisine requires a multitude of spices to develop rich, complex flavors, so don't let this longer ingredient list deter you. However, one ingredient you won't see on this list? Eggs. I've replaced the traditional meatball binder and moisture provider with a much more flavorful alternative: cinnamon applesauce. It does double duty on the taste and texture fronts. To streamline your prep, the meatballs bake in the oven while you make the sauce on the stove top. Blending the sauce isn't essential, but it does lead to a velvety smooth texture.

PREP	30 minutes
COOK	35 minutes
Yield	*4 servings*

FOR THE MEATBALLS

Cooking spray

1 slice white bread, roughly torn

2 tablespoons heavy cream

1 pound ground chicken or turkey

¼ cup cinnamon applesauce

1 tablespoon tomato paste

2 tablespoons minced fresh cilantro

½ teaspoon kosher salt

¼ teaspoon black pepper

FOR THE SAUCE

2 tablespoons extra-virgin olive oil

1 cup diced yellow onion (1 onion)

1 tablespoon minced garlic

2 teaspoons minced fresh ginger

2 tablespoons tomato paste

2 tablespoons water

1 (15-ounce) can tomato sauce

2 tablespoons sugar

1 tablespoon garam masala

2 teaspoons turmeric

2 teaspoons smoked paprika

1 teaspoon ground cumin

½ teaspoon ground cinnamon

1 teaspoon kosher salt, plus more for seasoning

2 cups heavy cream

Black pepper, for seasoning

Minced fresh cilantro, for garnish

Cooked basmati rice or naan, for serving

MAKE THE MEATBALLS Preheat the oven to 400°F. Grease a 13x9-inch baking pan with cooking spray.

In a small bowl, combine the bread and cream. Let the mixture sit for 5 minutes, then mash it with a fork.

In a medium bowl, combine the bread mixture, ground chicken, applesauce, tomato paste, cilantro, salt, and pepper. Using your hands, mix just until combined. Scoop out 1½-tablespoon portions of the mixture and roll into balls, then arrange them in a single layer in the baking dish.

continued

Bake the meatballs until they are cooked through, about 20 minutes. While the meatballs bake, make the sauce.

MAKE THE SAUCE Add the olive oil to a large heavy-bottomed stockpot set over medium-low heat. Add the onion, garlic, and ginger and cook, stirring, until the onion is translucent, 5 to 7 minutes. Add the tomato paste and cook, stirring, until caramelized, about 3 minutes. Stir in the water, scraping up any brown bits on the bottom of the pan. Stir in the tomato sauce, sugar, garam masala, turmeric, paprika, cumin, cinnamon, and salt and cook for 5 minutes.

If desired, transfer the sauce to a blender and blend until pureed, then return to the stockpot. Whisk in the cream then simmer the sauce until it has thickened slightly, about 15 minutes, stirring occasionally. Taste and season the sauce with salt and pepper.

Add the meatballs to the sauce, stirring gently to combine.

Garnish the meatballs with cilantro, then serve with basmati rice or naan.

Chicken Pot Pie with Cheesy Drop Biscuits

Chicken pot pie is the king of comfort food. A single scoop of this hearty meal is enough to warm you even on the coldest of days. All of the usual suspects are here, plus a newcomer: chipotles in adobo. They lend subtle spice to the filling and are backed up with cumin, fresh oregano, corn, and lime juice to give this casserole a Southwestern spin. One more twist comes in the form of the topping. I've never been a fan of delicate puff pastry when it comes to pot pie, so it's cheesy chive drop biscuits to the rescue.

PREP	30 minutes
COOK	55 minutes
Yield	*8 servings*

FOR THE FILLING

½ cup (1 stick) unsalted butter

1 cup diced onion (1 onion)

½ cup diced peeled carrot

½ cup diced celery

1 tablespoon minced garlic

2 to 3 tablespoons finely chopped chipotles in adobo sauce

1 tablespoon minced fresh oregano

1½ teaspoons ground cumin

½ teaspoon kosher salt, plus more for seasoning

½ cup all-purpose flour

3½ cups chicken broth

1 cup heavy cream

4 cups cooked, shredded rotisserie chicken or turkey, skin and bones discarded (1 large chicken)

1½ cups frozen peas

1½ cups frozen corn kernels

2 tablespoons fresh lime juice

Black pepper, for seasoning

FOR THE BISCUITS

2 cups all-purpose flour

2 teaspoons baking powder

1 teaspoon baking soda

½ teaspoon kosher salt

¼ teaspoon black pepper

2 cups shredded cheddar cheese

6 tablespoons (¾ stick) cold unsalted butter, cubed

1¼ cups buttermilk

2 tablespoons chopped fresh chives

MAKE THE FILLING Melt the butter in a large heavy-bottomed stockpot or Dutch oven set over medium-low heat. Add the onion, carrot, celery, garlic, chipotles, oregano, cumin, and salt. Cook, stirring occasionally, until the vegetables are tender, about 10 minutes. Sprinkle the flour over the vegetables and cook, stirring constantly, for 2 minutes.

continued

Stir in the broth and cream, scraping up any brown bits from the bottom of the pot. Bring the mixture to a boil, then reduce to a simmer and cook until thickened slightly, about 3 minutes.

Stir in the chicken, peas, corn, and lime juice, then taste and season with salt and pepper.

Transfer the filling to a 13x9-inch baking dish and place the baking dish on a baking sheet.

MAKE THE BISCUITS Preheat the oven to 400°F.

In a large bowl, sift together the flour, baking powder, baking soda, salt, and pepper. Stir in the shredded cheese. Add the butter and use your hands to gently mix it all together, working the butter into the flour with your fingers. Stir in the buttermilk and chives, mixing just until combined.

Using two spoons, drop the biscuit dough onto the pot pie filling in eight large mounds. Bake the pot pie until the filling is bubbling and the biscuits are golden brown and puffed, 30 to 35 minutes.

Remove the pot pie from the oven and let it stand for 10 minutes before serving.

Kelly's Note ∗ *Opt for store-bought rotisserie chicken or swap in leftover turkey to make the most of holiday extras.*

Baked Chicken Tenders with Honey Mustard Sauce

Secret ingredient

Crispy Rice Cereal

A household with three boys under age 5 equals a whole lot of chicken tenders, so I've become an expert in the art of finger-friendly poultry options. When I don't have traditional breadcrumbs on hand, I raid the pantry for any variety of cereal that I (or more commonly, the boys) can pulverize into a coating. Getting the kids in on the cooking action is one way to guarantee zero protests come dinner time. If they've made it, they're way more likely to eat it!

PREP	15 minutes
COOK	15 minutes
Yield	*4 servings*

FOR THE HONEY MUSTARD SAUCE

½ cup mayonnaise

3 tablespoons honey

2 tablespoons Dijon mustard

1 tablespoon fresh lemon juice

½ teaspoon kosher salt, plus more for seasoning

⅛ teaspoon paprika

FOR THE CHICKEN TENDERS

Cooking spray

½ cup all-purpose or whole wheat flour

1 teaspoon kosher salt

¼ teaspoon black pepper

2 large eggs

4 cups crispy rice cereal, crushed (see Kelly's Note)

1¼ pounds chicken tenders, tendons removed

MAKE THE SAUCE In a small bowl, whisk together the mayonnaise, honey, mustard, lemon juice, salt, and paprika. Taste and season with more salt if needed.

MAKE THE CHICKEN TENDERS Preheat the oven to 475°F. Line a baking sheet with foil and coat it generously with cooking spray.

In a shallow bowl, whisk together the flour, salt, and pepper. In a second shallow bowl, whisk the eggs together with 3 tablespoons of the honey mustard sauce, then cover and refrigerate the remaining sauce. In a third shallow bowl, spread out the crushed cereal.

Dredge one of the chicken tenders in the flour mixture, then dip it into the egg mixture, shaking off any excess. Immediately add it to the bowl with the cereal, pressing the cereal firmly onto all sides, then place the tender on the baking sheet. Repeat the breading process with the remaining tenders, spacing them 1 inch apart on the sheet.

Spray the tenders with cooking spray. Bake for 15 minutes, flipping them once halfway through, until the chicken is cooked through and crispy.

Remove the chicken tenders from the oven and serve with the honey mustard sauce for dipping.

Kelly's Note * *The cleanest way to get kids in on the cereal crushing is to seal it in a plastic bag, hand them a measuring cup, and let them whack away.*

Inside-Out Grilled Ham and Cheese

It's a beautiful thing when garlic bread and grilled cheese become BFFs: You get the best of both carb worlds. Invite ham to the party and you've suddenly turned a side dish into a 20-minute meal. Consider this recipe a template that you can customize with any combination of bread, cheese, and meat. The DIY garlic butter and crunchy Parmesan coating will get friendly with all pairings, from turkey and Swiss on brioche to roast beef and cheddar on rye, so don't hesitate to use whatever you have in your fridge.

PREP	10 minutes
COOK	20 minutes
Yield	*4 servings*

½ cup (1 stick) unsalted butter, at room temperature

2 tablespoons minced garlic

2 teaspoons chopped fresh chives

¼ teaspoon black pepper

8 slices sourdough bread

⅔ cup freshly grated Parmesan cheese

4 slices provolone cheese

2 cups shredded Gruyère cheese

8 thin slices ham

In a small bowl, stir together the butter, garlic, chives, and pepper. Divide the garlic butter among the slices of bread, spreading it in an even layer on one side of each slice. Sprinkle the Parmesan cheese atop the garlic butter, pressing it firmly into the bread.

Assemble each sandwich by placing a slice of provolone on a non-coated side of one slice of bread. Sprinkle the Gruyère on top. Add two slices of ham, then place a second slice of bread on top with the coated side facing up.

Cook the sandwiches one at a time in a small nonstick skillet set over medium-low heat until the Parmesan cheese melts and becomes crispy, about 2 minutes. Flip the sandwich once, cover the pan with a lid, and continue cooking until the interior cheeses have melted and the bottom side of the sandwich is golden brown and crispy, about 3 minutes longer.

Remove the sandwich from the skillet, then slice and serve.

B.L.T.P. Sandwich

Secret ingredient

Pimento Peppers

One of my favorite hospitality groups, Hillstone Restaurant Group, serves the most incredible pimento cheese dip at several of their locations, including R+D Kitchen in Newport Beach, California, which is where I first sampled the dip. It's thick, creamy, cheesy, and served with warm tortilla chips. While it's great for dipping, it's even better for sandwiching. Here, classic mayo got the cut, and DIY pimento cheese became the star of this B.L.T. (and then some) show.

PREP	10 minutes
COOK	10 minutes
Yield	*4 servings*

FOR THE PIMENTO CHEESE

4 ounces cream cheese, at room temperature

2 cups shredded sharp cheddar cheese

¼ cup mayonnaise

2 tablespoons diced jarred pimento peppers

½ teaspoon kosher salt

¼ teaspoon black pepper

FOR THE SANDWICHES

8 slices thick-cut bacon

8 slices brioche bread

1 heart of romaine, halved, leaves separated

4 thick slices tomato

Kosher salt and black pepper

MAKE THE PIMENTO CHEESE In a medium bowl, combine the cream cheese, cheddar cheese, and mayonnaise. Using a spatula, stir until smooth and combined. Stir in the pimento peppers, salt, and pepper, then taste and season.

MAKE THE SANDWICHES Cook the bacon in a large skillet set over medium heat, draining the fat as needed, until crisped. Set the bacon aside.

Toast the bread.

To assemble each sandwich, spread a portion of the pimento cheese on one slice of bread. Top with romaine leaves and a slice of tomato. Sprinkle the tomato with salt and pepper, then arrange two slices of bacon on top. Add the top piece of bread, cut the sandwich in half, and serve.

Sweet Chili Pork Tenderloin

Pork tenderloin is one of the most overlooked proteins in existence. Pork chops and pork belly always have a place in the spotlight, while the humble tenderloin rarely makes it onto a menu. Not in our house! It's the second most-requested recipe from my husband (see page 184 for number 1), so it pops up on the weekly rotation year-round. It only requires a handful of ingredients, mostly because Chinese five-spice powder is, exactly as its name states, five flavor-packed spices in one. Best of all, adding the tenderloin to a preheated pan guarantees that heavenly crust without having to sear it on the stovetop before finishing it in the oven. It's a technique two-fer!

PREP	10 minutes
COOK	25 minutes
Yield	*4 servings*

3 cloves garlic, peeled

½ teaspoon kosher salt

1 tablespoon Chinese five-spice powder

1½ teaspoons rice vinegar

1½ teaspoons extra-virgin olive oil

1 (1¼-pound) pork tenderloin

2 tablespoons vegetable oil

Thai sweet chili sauce, for serving

Coconut Rice (page 188), for serving

Place a cast-iron skillet or large ovenproof skillet in the oven, then preheat the oven to 450°F.

Finely mince the garlic, then sprinkle the salt on top. Use the flat side of a knife to mash the garlic into a paste. Add the garlic paste to a small bowl, then stir in the five-spice powder, vinegar, and olive oil. Trim off any silverskin from the tenderloin, then thoroughly dry it. Rub the spice mixture all over the tenderloin.

Once the oven reaches 450°F, carefully remove the skillet and add the vegetable oil, swirling to coat the bottom of the pan. Add the tenderloin (bending it slightly into a "U" shape if needed), then immediately return the pan to the oven and bake the tenderloin for 10 minutes. Flip the tenderloin, then reduce the oven temperature to 400°F. Continue baking the tenderloin for 10 to 15 minutes, until it reaches an internal temperature of 145°F.

Transfer the tenderloin to a cutting board and immediately brush it generously with Thai sweet chili sauce. Cover the tenderloin loosely with foil and let it rest for 5 minutes.

Slice the tenderloin and serve with Coconut Rice and additional sweet chili sauce for dipping.

Sweet Heat Pepperoni Pizza

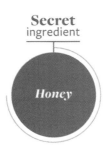

Secret ingredient

Honey

Searching for the best slice in New York City is an impossible feat, but I spent six years devoting myself to the cause. There's Roberta's, Nino's, Luigi's, and Joe's. Then there's Paulie Gee's, Di Fara, and Prince Street Pizza to name a few more, and we're barely starting to slice our way through the surface of all the five boroughs have to offer. Bottom line: Everyone will have a different opinion when it comes to the Big Apple's best pizza, but Emily in the West Village gets my vote. I'd even go one step further and claim their Colony pizza (pepperoni, pickled chili, and honey) as my all-time favorite pie. It's sweet, spicy, and ready for you to re-create in less time than it takes to get a table at Emily.

PREP	1 hour 15 minutes
COOK	10 minutes
Yield	*4 servings*

FOR THE DOUGH

Cooking spray

¾ cup water, heated to 110°F

1 (¼-ounce) packet active dry yeast

1 teaspoon honey

2 to 2¼ cups all-purpose flour, plus more for dusting work surface

2 tablespoons extra-virgin olive oil

1 teaspoon kosher salt

Cornmeal, for dusting baking sheet

FOR THE TOPPINGS

½ cup marinara sauce

8 ounces fresh mozzarella cheese, thinly sliced

⅓ cup sliced pepperoni

⅓ cup sliced pepperoncini

½ teaspoon dried oregano

Honey, for serving

MAKE THE DOUGH Grease a large bowl with cooking spray and set aside.

Combine the water, yeast, and honey in the bowl of a stand mixer fitted with the dough hook attachment. Let the mixture sit until the yeast becomes foamy, about 5 minutes. Add 2 cups flour, the olive oil, and salt. Mix on medium speed until the dough comes together into a ball, about 5 minutes. If the dough is still very sticky, add more flour as needed, 1 tablespoon at a time.

Lightly flour your work surface, then turn out the dough and knead it ten times. Transfer the dough to the greased bowl. Cover and let rest in a warm, dark place until it has doubled in size, about 1 hour.

Preheat the oven to 500°F. Dust a pizza stone or the bottom of a baking sheet generously with cornmeal.

Lightly flour your work surface. Turn out the dough and punch down with your hands to deflate. Using a rolling pin, roll the dough until it is ½ inch thick and about 12 inches in diameter. Transfer the dough onto the prepared pizza stone or baking sheet.

TOP THE PIZZA Spread the marinara sauce on top of the dough, leaving a 1-inch border around the edges. Arrange the mozzarella cheese, pepperoni, and pepperoncini on top. Bake the pizza until the crust is baked through and crisped around the edges, about 10 minutes.

Remove the pizza from the oven. Sprinkle with oregano and drizzle with honey, then slice and serve.

Crispy Slow Cooker Carnitas (recipe, page 176)

Crispy Slow Cooker Carnitas

Secret ingredient

Cocoa Powder

A single step is all that separates you from mediocre I-still-prefer-restaurant carnitas and spectacular mine-are-better-than-restaurant carnitas. It all comes down to the oven. So, yes, while this is a tried-and-true slow cooker recipe, you do not want to skip the final step of crisping up the shredded pork under the broiler. It provides a bit of crunch and intensifies the chocolatey dry rub. Cocoa and pork are an unordinary pairing that leads to extraordinary flavor. Add orange juice and beer to the equation and the only decision left is whether you're going to serve your restaurant-worthy carnitas piled into tortillas, sealed into quesadillas, or scooped atop salads. (*Pictured on the preceding pages, 174–175.*)

PREP	15 minutes
COOK	8 minutes
Yield	*6 servings*

1 (3- to 4-pound) boneless, skinless pork shoulder, trimmed

4 cloves garlic, minced

2 tablespoons unsweetened cocoa powder

2 teaspoons ground cumin

2 teaspoons dried oregano

1 teaspoon chili powder

1 tablespoon kosher salt, plus more for seasoning

1 teaspoon black pepper

1 medium white onion, roughly chopped

2 bay leaves

12 ounces Mexican beer, such as Pacífico

1 cup orange juice

2 tablespoons fresh lime juice, plus more for seasoning

Cooking spray

Pat the pork shoulder dry with paper towels and rub the minced garlic all over.

In a medium bowl, whisk together the cocoa, cumin, oregano, chili powder, salt, and pepper. Rub the spice mixture all over the pork, then place it in the slow cooker.

Scatter the onion and bay leaves around the pork, then add the beer, orange juice, and lime juice. Cover the slow cooker and set it to Low for 8 hours or High for 5 hours. When done, the pork should be cooked through and tender enough to shred with two forks.

Arrange an oven rack about 4 inches from the broiler, then preheat the oven to broil. Line a rimmed baking sheet with foil, then coat it with cooking spray.

Transfer the pork to a cutting board and reserve the juices in the slow cooker. Using two forks, shred the pork. Transfer the shredded pork onto the prepared baking sheet and drizzle with ¾ cup of the juices from the slow cooker. Broil the carnitas until it is slightly crispy, stirring as needed, about 5 minutes.

Taste and season the carnitas with additional salt and lime juice, then serve.

Sunday Short Rib Ragù with Polenta

Secret
ingredient

Bittersweet Chocolate

It is low and slow for the win in this impossibly tender and rich short rib ragù. The secret ingredient gets its inspiration from Mexican mole, where bittersweet chocolate lends subtle sweetness while cutting down on the acidity of the tomatoes. This is a hearty, stick-to-your-ribs (pun intended) meal that is well worth the time and effort. I serve it atop creamy Parmesan polenta, but there are no rules when it comes to ragù. Mashed potatoes, spaghetti squash, and sautéed greens would all welcome a scoop or two of this Sunday sauce.

PREP	25 minutes
COOK	3 hours 45 minutes
Yield	*6 servings*

FOR THE RAGÙ

2½ pounds bone-in beef short ribs

Kosher salt and black pepper, for seasoning

2 tablespoons vegetable oil

2 cups diced yellow onions (2 onions)

1 cup diced peeled carrots

1 cup diced celery

1 tablespoon minced garlic

3 tablespoons tomato paste

2 teaspoons minced fresh rosemary

1 cup red wine

2 cups beef broth

2 bay leaves

2 tablespoons unsalted butter, cold and cut into pieces

1½ ounces bittersweet chocolate, roughly chopped

Kosher salt and black pepper

FOR THE POLENTA

2 cups chicken broth

2 cups whole milk

½ teaspoon kosher salt, plus more for seasoning

1 cup polenta

½ cup freshly grated Parmesan cheese, plus more for serving

2 tablespoons unsalted butter, cut into pieces

¼ teaspoon black pepper

MAKE THE RAGÙ Pat the short ribs dry, then generously season with salt and pepper on all sides.

Heat the oil in a large heavy-bottom stockpot or Dutch oven set over medium-high heat. Once the oil is hot, brown the short ribs in batches, turning as needed. Transfer the short ribs to a plate and remove all but 2 tablespoons of the drippings.

Reduce the heat to medium, then add the onions, carrots, celery, and ½ teaspoon salt to the pot and cook, stirring, until the onions are translucent, about 7 minutes. Add the garlic and cook, stirring, for an additional 2 minutes.

Stir in the tomato paste and rosemary and cook, stirring, until the tomato paste begins to caramelize, about 2 minutes. Deglaze the pan with the red wine, scraping up any brown bits, and cook until the wine has reduced by half.

Stir in the beef broth and bay leaves, then return the short ribs and all juices to the pot, ensuring that the short ribs are completely submerged in the liquid. Bring the mixture to a boil, then reduce the heat to low and cover the pot. Simmer the ragù until the short ribs are fork-tender, about 3 hours.

continued

Transfer the short ribs to a cutting board. Discard the bones and any gristle, then use two forks to shred the meat.

MAKE THE POLENTA Combine the chicken broth, milk, and salt in a large saucepan set over medium heat. Bring the mixture to a boil, then gradually whisk in the polenta. Continue whisking constantly until the mixture is smooth and begins to thicken, about 3 minutes.

Reduce the heat to low and cook the polenta, whisking occasionally, until it is tender, 25 to 30 minutes. If at any point the polenta becomes too thick, whisk in ½ cup water at a time. Stir in the Parmesan cheese, butter, and pepper, then taste and season the polenta with salt.

FINISH THE RAGù Strain the sauce into a saucepan, using a spatula to firmly press the vegetables into the strainer to extract as much liquid as possible. Discard the vegetables and bay leaves.

Bring the sauce to a simmer and cook, skimming off the fat as needed, until it has reduced by half.

Return the shredded meat to the sauce, then stir in the butter and chocolate. Cook, stirring occasionally, for 5 minutes, until the butter and chocolate have melted, then taste and season with salt and pepper.

When ready to serve, divide the polenta into shallow bowls and spoon the ragù on top. Garnish with Parmesan cheese and serve.

Beef Bulgogi Lettuce Wraps

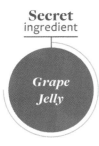

Secret ingredient

Grape Jelly

Mastering a marinade for all types of beef was one of my first big culinary achievements. It doesn't matter how inexpensive the cut is, if it bathes long enough in the perfect blend of savory, sour, sweet, and salty flavorings, then the result is always a win for Team Taste Buds. This is your all-purpose beef marinade, which works just as well for rib eye bulgogi as it would with flank steak or even kabobs. The traditional version of bulgogi marinade includes grated fresh pear, which lends a fruity sweetness to the umami-rich mixture of soy sauce, sesame oil, and chili paste. I'd argue that grape jelly takes the flavor up a notch, highlighting the uncommon but seriously underrated pairing of soy sauce and grapes. (*Pictured on the following pages, 180–181.*)

PREP	2 hours 30 minutes
COOK	10 minutes
Yield	*4 servings*

FOR THE BEEF

2 pounds boneless rib eye or top sirloin steaks

½ cup soy sauce

¾ cup grape jelly

1 tablespoon sesame oil

1 tablespoon chili garlic sauce or gochujang chili paste

¼ cup rice vinegar

2 tablespoons minced garlic

1 tablespoon minced fresh ginger

¼ cup thinly sliced shallots

2 tablespoons vegetable oil

FOR THE LETTUCE WRAPS

Peeled and shredded carrots

Sliced cucumbers

Bibb lettuce leaves

Sliced scallions

Sesame seeds

MAKE THE BEEF Wrap the steaks securely in plastic wrap, then place them in the freezer for 30 minutes (see Kelly's Note).

In a large bowl, whisk together the soy sauce, jelly, sesame oil, chili garlic sauce, vinegar, garlic, ginger, and shallots.

Remove the steaks from the freezer and discard the plastic wrap. Using a sharp knife, slice the steak into ⅛-inch-thick slices. Add the sliced steak to the bowl with the marinade and toss to combine. Cover the bowl with plastic wrap and refrigerate for a minimum of 2 hours, or up to overnight.

When ready to cook, heat the oil in a large skillet over high heat. Using a slotted spoon, transfer the beef to the pan. Cook, stirring quickly and constantly, until the beef is cooked through and caramelized slightly, about 10 minutes. Transfer the beef to a serving plate.

ASSEMBLE THE LETTUCE WRAPS To assemble, divide the beef, carrots, and cucumbers among the lettuce leaves. Garnish with scallions and sesame seeds and serve.

Kelly's Note ✳ *Freezing the steaks ensures that you can slice them very thinly, which means the meat will cook quickly and remain tender.*

Beef Bulgogi
Lettuce Wraps
(recipe, page 179)

French Onion Steak Sandwiches

Caramelized onions get my vote for Most Versatile Topping when it comes to elevating sandwiches, burgers, pizza, and even crostini. I've boosted the sweet, rich flavor of the onions with an entire package of onion soup mix; yes, that foil-lined packet loaded with powdered flavorings. Sautéing the seasonings with butter gives them new life, making these caramelized onions intensely flavorful and perfect for layering with thin slices of sirloin, melted Gruyère cheese, and peppery arugula tossed with fresh lemon juice and olive oil.

PREP	20 minutes
COOK	1 hour 20 minutes
Yield	*4 servings*

2 tablespoons unsalted butter

2 medium white onions, thinly sliced

1 (1-ounce) package onion soup mix

2 (8-ounce) sirloin steaks

Kosher salt and black pepper

Extra-virgin olive oil

4 French sandwich rolls, halved

1 cup shredded Gruyère cheese

1 tablespoon fresh lemon juice

2 cups arugula

Heat the butter in a large skillet set over medium heat. Once the butter has melted, add the onions and cook, stirring occasionally, for 20 minutes, until the onions soften and become golden. Reduce the heat to medium-low, then stir in the onion soup mix. Cook the onions, stirring as needed to prevent burning, until they are dark brown and caramelized, about an additional 30 minutes. If at any point the onions begin to burn, add 2 tablespoons water to the pan and continue cooking. Set the onions aside.

Season the steaks with salt and pepper. Coat the bottom of a large skillet set over medium-high heat with olive oil. Once the skillet is hot, add the steaks and cook to your desired doneness. For medium-rare, cook for about 8 minutes, or until they reach an internal temperature of 130°F.

Transfer the steaks to a cutting board and let them rest for 10 minutes. Slice the steaks as thinly as possible against the grain.

Preheat the oven to broil. Place the four bottom halves of the sandwich rolls on a baking sheet, then divide the onions among the rolls. Top the onions with the steak and Gruyère cheese. Place the sandwiches about 4 inches under the broiler and broil until the cheese is melted.

In a medium bowl, whisk together 2 teaspoons olive oil and the lemon juice. Add the arugula and a pinch of salt and pepper, then toss to combine. Top the sandwiches with the arugula, then add the top halves of the rolls and serve.

Julio's Flank Steak with Chimichurri Sauce

If my husband, Julio, had to name his favorite meal of all time, there would be zero hesitation before firmly stating, "flank steak with chimichurri sauce." While many steak lovers prefer pricier cuts of beef, he'd choose a flank steak over a filet any day of the week. I've upped the ante on the sauce by incorporating another one of his favorite foods: blistered shishito peppers. They join forces with the usual fresh herbs, garlic, citrus, and a squeeze of honey to create a mild, peppery chimichurri that can also serve as a marinade for all types of meats and veggies.

PREP	20 minutes
COOK	15 minutes
Yield	*4 servings*

1 tablespoon vegetable oil

4 ounces shishito peppers

½ cup lightly packed fresh Italian parsley leaves

½ cup lightly packed fresh cilantro leaves

1 tablespoon lightly packed fresh oregano leaves

1 tablespoon roughly chopped shallot

3 cloves garlic, peeled

2 tablespoons red wine vinegar

1 tablespoon fresh lime juice

2 teaspoons honey

¼ teaspoon kosher salt, plus more for seasoning

⅛ teaspoon black pepper, plus more for seasoning

⅓ cup extra-virgin olive oil

1 (2-pound) flank steak

Heat the vegetable oil in a skillet set over medium-high heat. Once the oil is hot, add the peppers and cook, turning occasionally, until blistered on all sides, about 5 minutes.

Transfer the peppers to a cutting board. Once they are cool enough to handle, slice off and discard the stems, then transfer the peppers to the bowl of a food processor.

Add the parsley, cilantro, oregano, shallot, garlic, vinegar, lime juice, honey, salt, and pepper to the food processor and pulse until roughly chopped. With the motor running, stream in the olive oil. Continue blending until combined, scraping down the sides as needed. Taste and season the chimichurri with salt and pepper, then set aside.

Preheat a grill or heat a stovetop grill pan over medium-high heat. If using a grill, lightly oil the grate.

Season the steak generously with salt and pepper. Place the steak on the grill and cook undisturbed for 6 minutes. Flip it once and continue cooking until it reaches your desired level of doneness. For medium-rare, cook the steak until it reaches an internal temperature of 130°F.

Transfer the steak to a cutting board, cover loosely with foil, and let rest for 10 minutes.

Slice the steak against the grain into thin strips. Top the steak with the chimichurri and serve.

SoCal Fish Tacos with Mango Salsa

Secret
ingredient

Tajín Seasoning

You may recognize it from the rim of your margarita, but now the chili-lime spice known as Tajín is going from your glass to your plate. For a native San Diegan, there are few recipes more important to master than flaky fish tacos. They are a Southern California staple, right alongside guacamole and salsa. Tajín, which is available in the spice aisle or produce section of major grocery stores, is a flavor powerhouse. Its sour flavor is the perfect accompaniment to sweet mango-avocado salsa and refreshing cumin-lime crema.

PREP	20 minutes
COOK	20 minutes
Yield	*4 servings*

FOR THE MANGO SALSA

2 cups diced mango (2 medium mangoes)

1 medium avocado, pitted, peeled, and diced

⅓ cup finely diced red onion

½ jalapeño, seeded and minced, or more to taste

¼ cup chopped fresh cilantro

2 tablespoons fresh lime juice

½ teaspoon kosher salt

FOR THE CREMA

½ cup sour cream

2 teaspoons fresh lime juice

¼ teaspoon ground cumin

1 teaspoon kosher salt

FOR THE FISH

2 pounds flaky white fish, such as halibut or cod

2 tablespoons extra-virgin olive oil

2 tablespoons Tajín seasoning

½ teaspoon kosher salt

———

Corn or flour tortillas, for serving

Shredded purple cabbage, for serving

Lime wedges, for serving

MAKE THE SALSA In a medium bowl, stir together the mango, avocado, red onion, jalapeño, cilantro, lime juice, and salt. Cover the bowl and refrigerate.

MAKE THE CREMA In a small bowl, stir together the sour cream, lime juice, cumin, and salt. Cover the bowl and refrigerate.

COOK THE FISH Preheat the oven to 375°F. Line a baking sheet with parchment paper.

Arrange the fish on the baking sheet and drizzle with the olive oil, using your fingers to spread it evenly all over the fish. Sprinkle the fish on both sides with the Tajín and salt.

Bake the fish until it is flaky and cooked through, 18 to 20 minutes, depending on the thickness of your fillets. Remove the fish from the oven, then, using a fork, flake it apart into pieces.

Assemble each taco by arranging two tortillas on top of each other. Add cabbage, flaked fish, and mango salsa on top. Drizzle with the crema and serve immediately with the lime wedges.

Glazed Sesame Salmon with Coconut Rice

Secret ingredient

Maple Syrup

There are a few foods I absolutely will not eat. Up until my late 20s, the food at the top of that list was salmon. My distaste for the fish was so deep that I couldn't even smell it without making the kind of face I usually only make after taking tequila shots. But something clicked one day: Salmon, when sourced properly and cooked correctly, is the ultimate entrée. This sesame-inspired spin features a garlicky soy marinade/sauce that's sweetened with maple syrup. Serve the glazed fillets over creamy coconut rice, which is also my go-to starchy base for Sticky Pineapple Chicken (page 158) and Sweet Chili Pork Tenderloin (page 171).

PREP	1 hour
COOK	20 minutes
Yield	*4 servings*

FOR THE SALMON

1 cup soy sauce

¾ cup rice vinegar

¾ cup maple syrup

1 tablespoon sesame oil

1 tablespoon minced garlic

1 tablespoon minced fresh ginger

4 (6-ounce) center-cut salmon fillets

Cooking spray

2 teaspoons cornstarch

1 tablespoon water

FOR THE RICE

1 (14-ounce) can unsweetened coconut milk

1¼ cups water

1½ teaspoons maple syrup

¼ teaspoon kosher salt

1½ cups uncooked jasmine rice

———

¼ cup sliced scallions, for garnish

1 teaspoon toasted white sesame seeds (see Toasting Nuts and Seeds, page 105), for garnish

MAKE THE SALMON In a medium bowl, whisk together the soy sauce, vinegar, maple syrup, sesame oil, garlic, and ginger. Pour half of the mixture into a sealable plastic bag and reserve the other half in the bowl. Add the salmon fillets to the plastic bag, seal it, and refrigerate for 30 minutes.

Preheat the oven to 400°F. Spray a 13x9-inch baking dish with cooking spray.

Remove the salmon fillets from the bag and arrange in the baking dish, then pour half of the marinade from the bag on top. (Discard the remaining marinade from the bag.) Bake the salmon until it is cooked through and reaches your desired level of doneness, 12 to 15 minutes.

Pour the reserved soy sauce mixture from the bowl into a small saucepan set over medium heat. Whisk together the cornstarch with the water, then whisk the cornstarch mixture into the sauce. Bring the

continued

mixture to a boil, then reduce to a simmer and cook until it is thick enough to coat the back of a spoon, about 5 minutes.

Remove the salmon from the oven and brush with the glaze.

MAKE THE RICE In a medium saucepan, whisk together the coconut milk, water, maple syrup, and salt. Stir in the rice and bring it to a boil. Cover the saucepan, reduce the heat, and simmer until the rice is tender and all of the liquid is absorbed, about 20 minutes.

Fluff the rice with a fork, then spoon it onto serving plates. Top with the salmon fillets, then garnish with the scallions and sesame seeds and serve.

Kelly's Note * *To save time, make the coconut rice while the salmon is marinating.*

Shrimp and Three-Cheese Grits

Secret ingredient

Tequila

Shrimp and grits has always been one of those restaurant meals I never dreamed of re-creating at home. It seemed unreasonable to attempt to match the iconic flavor and texture that a team of professional chefs could whip up in minutes. But nothing is impossible with a little tequila! I've added a Southwestern spin to this classic Southern dish. The combination of sharp cheddar, Monterey Jack, and cream cheese guarantees your grits will be both flavorful and creamy, while a quick-fix taco seasoning joins forces with tequila to ensure your shrimp pack a citrusy, garlicky punch.

PREP	20 minutes
COOK	25 minutes
Yield	*4 to 6 servings*

FOR THE GRITS

2 cups whole milk

2 cups chicken broth

1 cup grits

½ teaspoon kosher salt, plus more for seasoning

¾ cup shredded sharp cheddar cheese

¾ cup shredded Monterey Jack cheese

2 ounces cream cheese

FOR THE SHRIMP

1 pound medium shrimp, peeled and deveined, tails removed

½ teaspoon ground cumin

½ teaspoon chili powder

½ teaspoon kosher salt

2 tablespoons extra-virgin olive oil

2 teaspoons minced garlic

½ cup silver tequila

3 tablespoons fresh lime juice

2 tablespoons chopped fresh cilantro

MAKE THE GRITS In a medium saucepan, combine the milk and broth. Bring the mixture to a boil over medium-high heat, then reduce the heat to medium and quickly whisk in the grits and salt. Whisk continuously for 2 minutes to prevent lumps from forming, then cook the grits, stirring frequently, until smooth and tender, about 25 minutes.

Remove the grits from the heat and immediately stir in the cheddar, Monterey Jack, and cream cheese. Taste and season the grits with salt, then set them aside.

MAKE THE SHRIMP In a large bowl, sprinkle the shrimp with the cumin, chili powder, and salt and toss to combine.

Heat the olive oil in a large nonstick skillet set over medium heat. Add the shrimp and cook, undisturbed, for 2 minutes. Flip the shrimp, then add the garlic and cook for an additional 1 minute. Add the tequila and cook until most of the liquid has evaporated. Stir in the lime juice and cilantro, then remove the shrimp from the heat.

Divide the grits among serving bowls. Top with the shrimp and serve immediately.

Nutty Ramen Noodles with Shrimp

Picking a favorite entrée in this cookbook is akin to naming a favorite child. I just can't do it. But let's say I had to list a few of my seafood favorites in no particular order, and then narrow down those select few to, say, a single choice. I'd land here, on Nutty Ramen Noodles with Shrimp. Perhaps it's the nostalgia for eating packaged ramen noodle soup as a child, or maybe it's the familiar flavor tie-ins with peanut sauce, which I could drink with a straw. Regardless of what draws me in, this dish is a lunch, dinner, and leftovers slam dunk. Pairing almond butter with coconut milk leads to an intensely creamy, nutty sauce that perfectly coats the curly carbs, tender shrimp, and crunchy almonds.

PREP	25 minutes
COOK	20 minutes
Yield	*4 servings*

3 (3-ounce) packages ramen noodles, seasoning packets discarded

2 tablespoons extra-virgin olive oil

½ cup diced white onion

1½ tablespoons minced garlic

½ teaspoon kosher salt

1 pound medium shrimp, shelled and deveined, tails removed

1 tablespoon sambal oelek

1 cup unsweetened coconut milk

⅓ cup almond butter

2 tablespoons sugar

2 tablespoons soy sauce

2 tablespoons fresh lime juice

Sliced scallions, for serving

Toasted sliced almonds, for serving (see Toasting Nuts and Seeds, page 105)

Bring a large pot of salted water to a boil. Add the ramen noodles and cook until tender, about 4 minutes. Drain the noodles and set aside.

Heat the oil in a large skillet set over medium heat. Add the onion, garlic, and salt and cook, stirring, until the onion is translucent, about 5 minutes. Add the shrimp and cook them undisturbed for 2 minutes. Flip them once and continue cooking until pink and cooked through, an additional 2 minutes. Using tongs, transfer the shrimp to a plate, leaving any juices in the pan.

Add the sambal oelek to the skillet and cook, stirring, for 2 minutes. Add the coconut milk, bring the mixture to a boil, and cook for 2 minutes. Reduce the heat to low, then whisk in the almond butter, sugar, soy sauce, and lime juice. Turn off the heat, then add the noodles and shrimp and toss to combine.

Transfer the noodles and shrimp to serving plates, top with scallions and slivered almonds, and serve.

Seared Scallops with Basil Risotto

Secret
ingredient

*Pineapple
Juice*

There's just something about the caramelized crust and meaty interior of scallops that makes them the perfect protein. They also have a naturally delicate flavor, so it's important to let them shine with a simple seasoning of salt and pepper. However, that means whatever scallops are served with has to take the lead with big, bold taste. Cue basil-pineapple risotto! Once you make risotto with pineapple juice, you'll be hard pressed to go without it ever again. If you're looking to wow guests with a meal they'd be likely to find in a five-star restaurant, then this is your dish.

PREP	15 minutes
COOK	45 minutes
Yield	*4 servings*

2 cups pineapple juice

1½ cups vegetable broth

3 tablespoons unsalted butter

⅓ cup minced yellow onion

1 tablespoon minced garlic

1¼ cups uncooked Arborio rice

¾ cup freshly grated Parmesan cheese

½ teaspoon kosher salt, plus more for seasoning

¼ teaspoon black pepper, plus more for seasoning

3 tablespoons minced fresh basil

1 pound sea scallops

2 tablespoons vegetable oil, plus more as needed

½ cup microgreens, for serving

Combine the pineapple juice and broth in a medium saucepan set over medium heat. Bring the mixture to a simmer, then cover with a lid and remove from the heat.

Heat the butter in a large saucepan set over medium-low heat. Add the onion and garlic and cook, stirring, until the onion is translucent, about 5 minutes. Add the rice and cook, stirring, for 1 minute.

Add a ladle of the hot juice mixture to the saucepan and cook, stirring, until the liquid is fully absorbed. Continue adding the hot liquid to the saucepan, one ladle at a time and stirring intermittently, until the rice is no longer crunchy, about 30 minutes.

Stir in the Parmesan cheese, salt, and pepper, then turn off the heat and stir in the basil. Set aside, covered, while you cook the scallops.

Pat the scallops dry, then season with salt and pepper. Heat the oil in a medium skillet set over medium-high heat. Once the oil is hot, add half the scallops and cook undisturbed for 2 minutes. Flip the scallops once, then tilt the skillet and baste them with the oil. Continue cooking the scallops an additional 1 minute, until no longer translucent. Transfer to a plate and repeat with the remaining scallops, adding more oil as needed.

Divide the risotto among serving plates and top with the scallops. Garnish with microgreens and serve.

Fried Eggs and Rice

Secret ingredient

Wild Rice

Fried rice is my favorite way to pack as many veggies and proteins into a single meal while dirtying the least number of dishes. It also can be customized based on whatever you already have in your fridge or pantry, and it tastes great as leftovers. You can't ask for much more from a humble rice dish! I've swapped out white rice for wild rice, which is much less starchy (read: no gloppy mess), a bit crunchier in bite, and technically a type of grass, not grain. Top off your bowl with a fried egg or two, then break the yolk and give it all a stir.

PREP	20 minutes
COOK	55 minutes
Yield	*4 servings*

2 cups chicken broth

1 cup uncooked wild rice

3 tablespoons unsalted butter, divided, plus more as needed for frying eggs

1 teaspoon sesame oil

1 tablespoon minced garlic

2 teaspoons minced fresh ginger

¼ cup chopped scallions, plus more for serving

1 cup frozen peas and carrots, thawed

1 tablespoon soy sauce

1 teaspoon fish sauce (optional)

4 to 8 large eggs

Sesame seeds, for serving

In a medium saucepan set over medium heat, combine the broth and wild rice. Bring the mixture to a boil, then cover and reduce to a simmer. Cook the rice until no longer crunchy, about 45 minutes. Transfer the rice to a baking sheet lined with parchment paper or wax paper and spread into an even layer. Let the rice cool completely at room temperature or in the fridge.

Heat 1 tablespoon of the butter and the sesame oil in a large nonstick sauté pan set over medium heat. Add the garlic, ginger, and scallions and cook, stirring, until golden brown, about 3 minutes. Add the rice, peas and carrots, soy sauce, and fish sauce (if using) and cook, stirring, until combined. Remove the rice from the heat.

Heat the remaining 2 tablespoons butter in a large nonstick skillet set over medium-high heat. Once the butter has melted, crack four eggs into the skillet and fry to your desired doneness. Remove the eggs from the skillet then add more butter and fry additional eggs as desired.

Divide the rice among serving plates, then top with fried eggs. Garnish with chopped scallions and sesame seeds and serve.

Kelly's Note ⁎ *I'm a huge fan of frozen, precut veggies. They're just as nutritious as fresh varieties and help cut down on dinner prep time.*

Clean-Out-the-Fridge Frittata

Consider this a template for all of those leftover odds and ends in your fridge and pantry. The recipe is intentionally generic. Use your dairy, meat, and cheeses of choice, but follow these simple rules: Dairy should be full fat (think heavy cream, sour cream, cream cheese, or whole milk); meat should be precooked (think lunch meat, leftover bacon, or rotisserie chicken); and veggies should also be precooked to keep excess water from diluting the frittata. Be sure to stir a few dashes of tangy Worcestershire sauce into the eggs to cut the heaviness of the eggs and fillings, and breakfast, lunch, or dinner is done!

PREP	10 minutes
COOK	35 minutes
Yield	*4 servings*

12 large eggs

⅓ cup dairy

2 tablespoons Worcestershire sauce

Kosher salt and black pepper, for seasoning

2 tablespoons unsalted butter

2 cups diced cooked vegetables

1 cup diced cooked meat

1 cup shredded or crumbled cheese

2 tablespoons chopped fresh herbs, for serving

Preheat the oven to 350°F.

In a large bowl, whisk together the eggs, dairy, and Worcestershire. Season with salt and pepper.

Heat the butter in a large ovenproof nonstick sauté pan or cast-iron skillet set over medium heat. When the butter has melted, add the diced vegetables and cook, stirring, until warmed through, then stir in the diced meat. Add the egg mixture and let cook for 2 minutes. Then, using a rubber spatula, gently lift up the eggs and tilt the pan so that the uncooked eggs flow beneath.

Transfer the pan to the oven and bake the frittata for 20 to 30 minutes, depending on thickness, until the eggs are fully cooked. Sprinkle the cheese atop the frittata, then continue baking until the cheese is melted, about 3 minutes.

Remove the frittata from the oven and top with the herbs. Slice into wedges and serve.

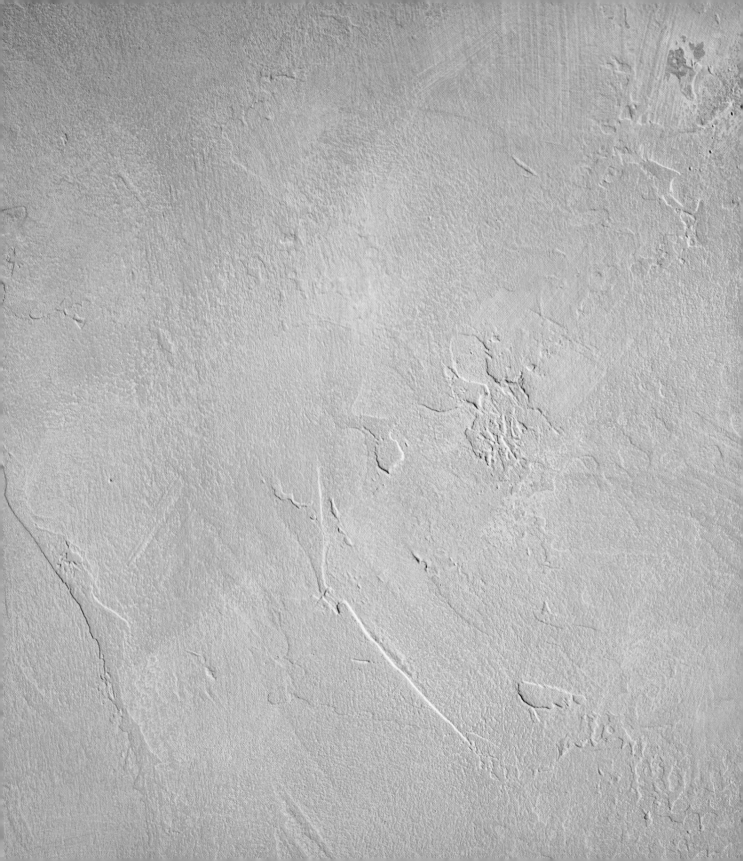

Sides

Smashed Patatas Bravas (recipe, page 207)

Confetti Corn Succotash

Edamame is a food group in our house. I buy the soybeans frozen and already shelled, which means I can get them on the boys' dinner plates in mere minutes. They're the perfect protein-packed food for little fingers. While the boys love them simply steamed, if time permits, the edamame take on the role of lima beans in this rainbow succotash. Bacon, garlic, and soy sauce make this a side for all of the senses, lending salty crunch to every colorful bite.

PREP	15 minutes
COOK	20 minutes
Yield	*6 servings*

6 slices bacon, cut into ½-inch pieces

2 teaspoons minced garlic

2 cups fresh or thawed frozen corn kernels

2 cups shelled edamame

1 cup diced red bell pepper

1 cup diced orange bell pepper

2 teaspoons soy sauce

½ teaspoon black pepper

Cook the bacon in a large skillet set over medium heat until all of the fat has rendered. Using a slotted spoon, transfer the bacon to a plate and discard all but 2 tablespoons of drippings from the skillet.

Add the garlic to the skillet and cook, stirring, until golden brown, about 2 minutes. Add the corn, edamame, red bell pepper, orange bell pepper, soy sauce, and black pepper. Cook, stirring occasionally, until the peppers have softened slightly, about 5 minutes.

Return the cooked bacon to the skillet and stir to combine. Serve warm or at room temperature.

Drew's Ultimate Dinner Rolls

Secret ingredient

Orange

My dad, Drew, was born in Budapest, Hungary, and immigrated to the U.S. in 1956, during the Hungarian Revolution. He learned to speak English by watching Wonder Bread commercials, so it's no small coincidence that one of his all-time favorite foods is bread—freshly baked bread, to be exact. Growing up in the States, he'd receive the same Christmas present every year: a single navel orange. This recipe is an ode to my dad and combines his two loves, with oranges lending faint citrus flavor to the lightest, fluffiest dinner rolls. I use the word "ultimate" sparingly when it comes to recipes, but this one is more than worthy of that claim.

PREP	1 hour 45 minutes
COOK	25 minutes
Yield	*12 rolls*

2¼ cups all-purpose flour, divided, plus more as needed

½ cup whole milk, warmed to 110°F

1 teaspoon grated orange zest

¼ cup fresh orange juice, warmed to 110°F

1 large egg, at room temperature

2 tablespoons unsalted butter, melted, plus more for topping

2 tablespoons sugar

1 (¼-ounce) packet instant (rapid rise) yeast

½ teaspoon kosher salt

Cooking spray

Large-flake sea salt, for topping

In the bowl of a stand mixer fitted with the dough hook attachment, combine 1 cup of the flour with the milk, orange zest, orange juice, egg, butter, sugar, yeast, and kosher salt. Mix on low speed until the flour is incorporated, scraping down the sides of the bowl as needed. Increase the speed to medium and continue mixing the dough for 2 minutes.

Add another ½ cup of the flour and continue mixing until it is incorporated. Add the remaining ¾ cup flour and mix until combined and the dough begins to form a ball. The dough should be sticky but pulling away from the sides of the bowl. If it is too sticky, add more flour, 2 tablespoons at a time, as needed.

Lightly flour your work surface. Turn out the dough and knead until it comes together into a smooth ball, about 2 minutes. Transfer the dough to a greased bowl, cover the bowl with a towel, and let rest in a warm, dark place until the dough has doubled in size, about 1 hour.

Grease an 8-inch round baking dish with cooking spray. Divide the dough into 12 pieces. Roll each piece into a ball, then arrange the balls in a single layer in the prepared pan. Cover the pan with a towel, then return it to the warm, dark place for 30 minutes.

Preheat the oven to 375°F. Uncover the rolls, brush with additional melted butter, and sprinkle with sea salt. Bake until the rolls are golden brown and cooked through, 20 to 25 minutes. Remove the rolls from the oven, brush them again with melted butter, and serve warm.

Smashed Patatas Bravas

Secret ingredient

Sun-Dried Tomatoes

When I studied abroad in Seville, Spain, I lived off the crispy, aioli-topped potatoes known as *patatas bravas*. While traditionally deep-fried, I've gone the roasted route but still achieve the same characteristic crunch. Swapping small cubes for smashed whole red potatoes makes these *patatas* the perfect finger food. Dip and dunk the crunchy rounds in a smooth, smoked paprika aioli that gets extra tang from sun-dried tomatoes.

PREP	15 minutes
COOK	1 hour 10 minutes
Yield	*6 servings*

5 tablespoons extra-virgin olive oil, divided

2 pounds small red potatoes, scrubbed

Kosher salt and black pepper

1 cup mayonnaise

3 tablespoons roughly chopped sun-dried tomatoes

2 cloves garlic, peeled

2 teaspoons smoked paprika

2 dashes Tabasco hot sauce, or more to taste

1 tablespoon red wine vinegar

Add ½ tablespoon olive oil to each of two baking sheets and use a pastry brush or your fingers to coat each sheet with oil.

In a large stockpot, cover the potatoes completely with water and add 2 teaspoons salt. Bring to a boil over medium-high heat and cook until the potatoes are fork-tender, 25 to 30 minutes.

Drain the potatoes, then divide them between the baking sheets and let them cool until you can comfortably handle them.

Preheat the oven to 425°F.

Using a potato masher or the bottom of a glass greased with olive oil, press down firmly on each potato and smash until it is about ½ inch thick.

Brush the potatoes with the remaining 4 tablespoons olive oil, then sprinkle with salt and pepper. Roast the potatoes until they are golden brown and crispy, about 40 minutes, flipping them once halfway through.

While the potatoes are roasting, make the aioli. In the bowl of a food processor, combine the mayonnaise, sun-dried tomatoes, garlic, smoked paprika, hot sauce, vinegar, and ½ teaspoon salt. Blend the mixture until combined, then taste and season with salt and hot sauce, as desired.

Arrange the potatoes on a serving plate. Serve with the aioli for dipping.

Creamed Super Greens

Secret ingredient

Mascarpone Cheese

If you're going to eat your greens, they might as well be bathed in a creamy, garlicky cheese sauce, right? I think we can all agree that traditional creamed spinach is long overdue for an update. I've added kale and chard to the party, bringing the total super greens to a whopping 1½ pounds. As long as we're upping the ante on the leafy greens, we might as well replace the cream cheese with its richer, smoother cousin: mascarpone. The result is a versatile creamed veggie side that would be more than happy to accompany anything from steak or pork to chicken or seafood.

PREP	5 minutes
COOK	20 minutes
Yield	*6 servings*

3 tablespoons unsalted butter

8 ounces fresh spinach leaves

8 ounces kale leaves, roughly chopped

8 ounces chard leaves, roughly chopped

⅓ cup all-purpose flour

1½ cups whole milk

1 (8-ounce) package mascarpone cheese

1 tablespoon garlic powder

½ teaspoon kosher salt

1 teaspoon black pepper

1 cup freshly grated Parmesan cheese

Heat the butter in a large heavy-bottomed stockpot set over medium heat. Once the butter has melted, add the spinach, kale, and chard in batches. Cook, stirring, until the greens have wilted and most of the liquid has evaporated, about 10 minutes.

Stir in the flour, then stir in the milk, mascarpone cheese, garlic powder, salt, and pepper. Cook, stirring occasionally, until the mixture thickens slightly, about 5 minutes.

Stir in the Parmesan cheese, then taste and season with salt and pepper. Serve warm.

Caramelized Brussels Sprouts

The first time I tried the unlikely duo of Brussels sprouts and fish sauce was at Uchiko, a Japanese farmhouse-style restaurant in Austin, Texas. This is my spin on their famous dish, featuring crispy roasted Brussels sprouts tossed in a savory caramel sauce. When used correctly (and sparingly), fish sauce does not actually taste fishy. Here, it complements the sweet and sour flavor profile of the Japanese-inspired side dish. (*Pictured on the following pages, 210–211.*)

PREP	10 minutes
COOK	40 minutes
Yield	*4 servings*

1½ pounds Brussels sprouts

2 tablespoons extra-virgin olive oil

4 tablespoons unsalted butter

2 teaspoons minced garlic

½ teaspoon crushed red pepper flakes

⅓ cup packed brown sugar

⅓ cup fresh lime juice

2 tablespoons soy sauce

1 tablespoon fish sauce

½ teaspoon cornstarch mixed with 2 teaspoons water

Preheat the oven to 400°F.

Trim the ends of the Brussels sprouts, then halve them lengthwise. Scatter them on a baking sheet, drizzle with the olive oil, and toss to combine. Roast for about 35 minutes, until the sprouts are golden brown. While they are roasting, make the sauce.

Heat the butter in a small saucepan set over medium heat. Once melted, add the garlic and crushed red pepper flakes and cook, stirring, until fragrant, about 1 minute. Whisk in the brown sugar and cook, whisking occasionally, until the mixture is smooth, about 3 minutes. Whisk in the lime juice, soy sauce, and fish sauce, bring to a boil, and cook for 2 minutes. Whisk in the cornstarch mixture and boil until thick and syrupy, about 2 minutes.

Remove the Brussels sprouts from the oven and increase the oven temperature to 450°F. Drizzle the sprouts with the sauce and toss to combine. Return the Brussels sprouts to the oven and continue roasting until caramelized, about an additional 5 minutes. Serve warm.

Caramelized
Brussels Sprouts
(recipe, page 209)

Coconut and Sweet Potato Mash

If traditional mashed potatoes are becoming a tired part of your side dish lineup, then grab some coconut milk, lime juice, and fresh ginger for this Thai-ish spin. A stand mixer or handheld electric mixer yields the lightest, smoothest possible puree (without any gumminess in sight), but a potato masher will also work if you prefer a chunkier consistency. Pop any leftovers into an airtight container, then stash them in the freezer for up to 6 months.

PREP	15 minutes
COOK	20 minutes
Yield	*4 servings*

2 pounds sweet potatoes

2½ teaspoons kosher salt, divided, plus more for seasoning

½ cup unsweetened coconut milk

3 tablespoons maple syrup

2 teaspoons fresh lime juice

2½ teaspoons grated fresh ginger

¼ teaspoon black pepper

Peel the sweet potatoes and cut into 1-inch dice.

In a large stockpot, cover the sweet potatoes with water and add 2 teaspoons of the salt. Bring to a boil over medium-high heat, reduce the heat to a simmer, and cook until the sweet potatoes are fork-tender, 15 to 20 minutes.

Drain the sweet potatoes and transfer to the bowl of a stand mixer fitted with the paddle attachment. Add the coconut milk, maple syrup, lime juice, ginger, remaining ½ teaspoon salt, and the pepper. Mix on low speed until the mash reaches your desired texture.

Taste and season the potatoes with salt, then serve.

Crispy Potato Croquettes

Secret ingredient

Yellow Zucchini

If turning leftover mashed potatoes into inventive dishes was an Olympic sport, let's just say I'd be somewhere between Michael Phelps and Simone Biles. I've dreamt up more than a dozen ways to transform surplus spuds into something other than, well, surplus spuds. Deep-fried croquettes are at the top of the list. I've mixed in grated zucchini as a veggie surprise, but you can add whatever spare vegetable, meat, cheese, or herbs you have stashed in your fridge. Pro tip: Finely dice any add-ins to ensure your croquettes form cohesive balls and stay intact while frying.

PREP	10 minutes
COOK	8 minutes
Yield	*6 servings*

1 medium yellow zucchini

2 cups leftover mashed potatoes (see Kelly's Note)

2 large eggs, whisked

¼ cup chopped scallions

1 cup shredded cheddar cheese

1½ teaspoons garlic powder

½ teaspoon kosher salt, plus more for seasoning

¼ teaspoon black pepper

1½ cups finely ground breadcrumbs

Vegetable oil, for frying

Ranch dressing, for serving

● **EQUIPMENT**
Deep-fry thermometer

Grate the zucchini on the small holes of a box grater. Transfer to a towel and wring out as much liquid as possible. Measure out 1 lightly packed cup of zucchini and transfer to a large bowl.

Add the mashed potatoes, eggs, scallions, cheddar cheese, garlic powder, salt, and pepper to the zucchini.

Spread the breadcrumbs in a separate shallow bowl.

Pour about 3 inches of vegetable oil into a large heavy-bottomed stockpot. Attach the deep-fry thermometer to the pot and set over medium-high heat. Line a baking sheet with paper towels.

Using a large spoon, scoop out one 3-tablespoon portion of the mixture and roll it into a ball. Add the ball to the breadcrumbs, turning to coat. Repeat with the remaining mixture.

Once the oil reaches 360°F, add several croquettes to the pot and fry, turning occasionally, until golden brown on all sides, about 2 minutes. Using a slotted spoon, transfer the croquettes to the prepared baking sheet and immediately season with salt. Repeat the frying process with the remaining croquettes, ensuring that you do not overcrowd the pan and that you return the oil to 360°F between batches.

Serve the croquettes warm with ranch dressing for dipping.

Kelly's Note ＊ *Leftover mashed potatoes vary in consistency; smoother, thicker mashed potatoes work best for croquettes because they are easy to form into balls and hold their shape when frying.*

Garlicky Cheese Bread

Secret
ingredient

Mayonnaise

When it comes to garlic bread, my motto is "go big or go home," which is why this recipe is not for the calorie faint of heart. All of the delicious players are in attendance: bread, butter, garlic, cheese, and yes, mayonnaise. You may have heard of the sandwich spread working moisture wonders in chocolate cake, but now it's ready for a turn in the savory spotlight. It contributes a touch of tang without overpowering the mix of garlic, chives, and cheeses that make this bread a great stand-alone snack or accompaniment to pasta, soup, or salad.

PREP	10 minutes
COOK	10 minutes
Yield	*10 to 12 servings*

1 (1-pound) loaf bread, such as French, Italian, or sourdough

1 cup mayonnaise

½ cup (1 stick) unsalted butter, at room temperature

2 tablespoons chopped fresh chives, plus more for serving

1 tablespoon minced garlic

¼ teaspoon black pepper

½ cup shredded mozzarella cheese

½ cup freshly grated Parmesan cheese

Preheat the oven to 350°F. Line a baking sheet with foil or parchment paper.

Slice the loaf of bread in half lengthwise.

In a medium bowl, stir together the mayonnaise, butter, chives, garlic, and pepper. Once the mixture is smooth, stir in the mozzarella cheese and Parmesan cheese.

Spread the cheese mixture atop each half of bread, then place the bread on the prepared baking sheet.

Bake the bread for 7 minutes. Carefully arrange an oven rack about 4 inches from the top of the oven. Switch the oven to broil, then broil the bread for about 3 minutes, until golden brown and slightly crispy.

Remove the bread from the oven, top with additional chives, then slice and serve warm.

Honey-Roasted Cauliflower and Broccoli

Secret ingredient

Honey Mustard

I've dreamt up nearly every iteration of cauliflower and broccoli to try to keep things interesting at the dinner table. Fritters? Homerun! Tots? Always a family favorite. Mashed? Surprisingly successful. But more often than I care to admit, my meal prep time is cut to a frenzied 10 minutes, so it's a sheet pan and a store-bought condiment to the rescue. The cruciferous duo gets a quick toss in a honey mustard dressing, then it's off to the oven for a high-heat roast. Bonus: Leftovers make for a great addition to pasta, salad, or pizza.

PREP	10 minutes
COOK	40 minutes
Yield	*4 to 6 servings*

1 pound cauliflower florets

1 pound broccoli florets

¼ cup store-bought honey mustard

3 tablespoons fresh lemon juice

2 tablespoons extra-virgin olive oil

1½ teaspoons garlic powder

½ teaspoon kosher salt

¼ teaspoon black pepper

Preheat the oven to 375°F. Line a baking sheet with foil.

Combine the cauliflower and broccoli in a large bowl.

In a small bowl, whisk together the honey mustard, lemon juice, olive oil, garlic powder, salt, and pepper. Pour the dressing over the cauliflower and broccoli and toss well to combine. Arrange the vegetables in a single layer on the baking sheet.

Bake the vegetables for 30 to 40 minutes, until fork-tender and slightly crispy. Remove the vegetables from the oven and serve.

Favorite Rice with Crispy Shallots

Secret ingredient

Brown Butter

One of the most common questions I get about recipes on Just a Taste is, "What side dish would I serve with this?" Whether it's beef, chicken, pork, seafood, or a vegetarian main, a simple rice side dish is always the answer. This recipe comes from San Diego chef Peter Calley, who grew up eating what his family called "favorite rice." The goal here is to not overthink things; it's long-grain rice and chicken or veggie broth, along with brown butter. I've added homemade crispy shallots as a topping, and the result is an unfussy, always reliable side dish for any meal and every occasion.

PREP	5 minutes
COOK	50 minutes
Yield	*6 servings*

½ cup vegetable oil

2 medium shallots, sliced into ⅛-inch-thick rings

4 cups chicken or vegetable broth

2 cups uncooked long-grain white rice, rinsed and drained

½ cup (1 stick) unsalted butter

Line a plate with paper towels. Place a sieve over a heatproof bowl.

In a small saucepan, combine the vegetable oil and shallots. Cook over medium-low heat, separating the rings with a fork as needed, until the shallots are golden brown, 45 to 50 minutes. While the shallots cook, make the rice.

In a large saucepan set over high heat, combine the broth and rice. Bring to a boil, then cover the pot securely and reduce the heat to low. Simmer the rice, undisturbed, for 20 minutes, until tender. While the rice cooks, make the brown butter.

Heat the butter in a small saucepan set over medium heat. Cook, whisking occasionally, until the butter begins to brown and has a nutty aroma, about 5 minutes. Remove the pan from the heat and pour the butter into a large serving bowl.

Pour the shallots into the sieve to drain, then transfer to the paper towel–lined plate to soak up any excess oil.

Fluff the rice with a fork, then add it to the bowl with the butter and toss to combine. Garnish with the crispy shallots and serve.

Maple-Glazed Carrots

Glazed carrots are my idea of the perfect side dish. When done right, they're soft, yet still have a bit of bite, and they're sweet, but not *too* sweet. It's a fine line between whipping up a savory side dish and veggie candy. This recipe strikes that perfect balance, and it just so happens to be a mash-up of my favorite carrot sides from two San Diego restaurants, Manhattan of La Jolla and Herb & Wood. I've borrowed the sticky glaze from the former and adopted the salted pistachios from the latter. Deglaze with a bit of bourbon and the modest root veggie just got its best makeover yet.

PREP	10 minutes
COOK	17 minutes
Yield	*6 servings*

2 pounds carrots

¼ cup (½ stick) unsalted butter

¼ cup bourbon

⅓ cup maple syrup

½ teaspoon kosher salt

¼ teaspoon black pepper

¼ cup salted roasted pistachios, chopped

Peel the carrots, then cut them on the bias into ½-inch-thick rounds.

Heat the butter in a large heavy-bottomed stockpot set over medium-high heat. Once the butter has melted, add the carrots and cook, stirring occasionally, until most of the liquid has evaporated, 7 to 10 minutes.

Reduce the heat to medium-low, then add the bourbon. Cook, stirring occasionally, until the bourbon has almost completely evaporated, about 2 minutes. Increase the heat to high, add the maple syrup, and boil until the mixture is thick and syrupy and the carrots are tender, 3 to 5 minutes.

Remove the carrots from the heat and stir in the salt and pepper. Garnish with the chopped pistachios and serve.

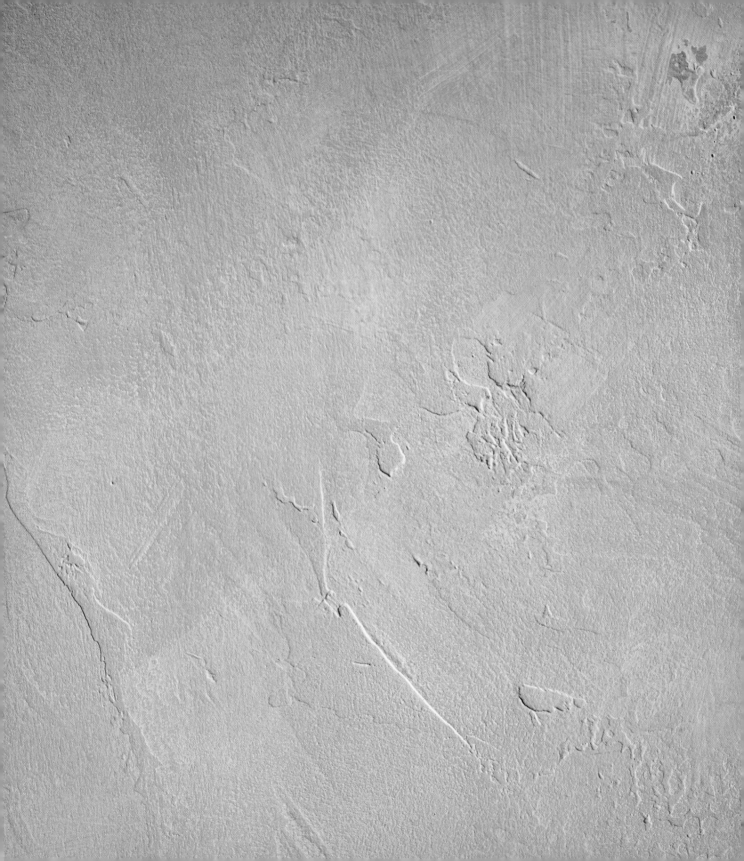

Desserts

The Chocolate
Chip Cookies
(recipe, page 224)

The Chocolate Chip Cookies

Secret
ingredient

Cream Cheese

It's the recipe that started it all. A classic confection with a creamy addition that yields my idea of the ultimate CCC: perfectly chewy centers that taper off into slightly crunchy edges. While there are a million and one chocolate chip cookie recipes out there, this one is a tried-and-tested five-star favorite with hundreds of thousands of loyal fans around the world. Secret ingredient aside, the real key to perfecting these cookies (and honestly, all cookies) is letting the dough firm up in the fridge before scooping and baking. The added chill time resolidifies the butter and ensures the texture will be spot-on. Grab the schmear and get mixing!

PREP	2 hours 20 minutes (including chilling)
COOK	15 minutes
Yield	*24 cookies*

2¼ cups all-purpose flour

1 teaspoon baking soda

1 teaspoon kosher salt

¾ cup (1½ sticks) unsalted butter, at room temperature

⅓ cup cream cheese, at room temperature

½ cup white sugar

1 cup packed light brown sugar

1½ teaspoons vanilla extract

2 large eggs, at room temperature

1 (12-ounce) package semisweet chocolate chips (2 cups)

Large-flake sea salt, for topping

Kelly's Note * *Store cooled cookies in an airtight container or sealable plastic bag at room temperature for up to 3 days.*

In a medium bowl, whisk together the flour, baking soda, and salt.

In the bowl of a stand mixer fitted with the paddle attachment, cream together the butter, cream cheese, white sugar, brown sugar, and vanilla extract until light and fluffy, about 2 minutes, scraping down the sides of the bowl as needed. Add the eggs, one at a time, beating well after each addition.

Add the flour mixture, beating just until combined, then add the chocolate chips and beat until combined.

Cover the bowl with plastic wrap and refrigerate the dough for a minimum of 2 hours or up to 3 days.

When ready to bake, preheat the oven to 375°F and line two baking sheets with parchment paper.

Drop 2-tablespoon mounds of dough onto the baking sheets, spacing them at least 2 inches apart. Bake the cookies for 12 to 15 minutes, rotating the baking sheets halfway through, until the cookies are golden brown on the edges but still slightly underbaked in the centers.

Remove the cookies from the oven and immediately sprinkle them with the sea salt. Cool the cookies on the baking sheets for 5 minutes then transfer to a wire rack to cool completely.

Chewy Oatmeal Raisin Cookies

When it comes to oatmeal cookies, are you Team Raisins or Team Chocolate Chips? Here's one team we can all be on: Team Chocolate-Covered Raisins. Lightly spiced oatmeal cookies get the best of both worlds in this recipe dreamt up by my brother, Grant. Whether you opt for milk or dark chocolate–covered raisins, the beauty of the candy is that the chocolate softens only slightly while in the oven, rather than melting into a mess. The result is soft and chewy cookies that just might sway chocolate chip devotees in the dried fruit direction.

PREP	10 minutes
COOK	15 minutes
Yield	*28 cookies*

1 cup (2 sticks) unsalted butter, at room temperature

1 cup packed light brown sugar

¾ cup white sugar

2 large eggs

1½ teaspoons vanilla extract

2½ cups old-fashioned oats

2 cups all-purpose flour

¾ teaspoon ground cinnamon

½ teaspoon kosher salt

1½ teaspoons baking powder

1 teaspoon baking soda

1 cup chocolate-covered raisins

Preheat the oven to 350°F. Line two baking sheets with parchment paper.

In the bowl of a stand mixer fitted with the paddle attachment, cream together the butter, brown sugar, and white sugar until light and fluffy, about 2 minutes. Add the eggs one at a time, beating between each addition, then beat in the vanilla extract.

Add the oats, flour, cinnamon, salt, baking powder, and baking soda and blend just until combined, then add the chocolate-covered raisins and mix until combined.

Spoon out 3-tablespoon mounds of the dough onto the baking sheets, spacing the mounds at least 2 inches apart.

Bake the cookies until they are pale golden and just begin to crisp around the edges, 12 to 15 minutes. Remove them from the oven and let cool for 5 minutes on the baking sheets before transferring to a wire rack to cool completely.

Shortcut Black and White Cookies

Secret ingredient

Cake Mix

New York City is home to some of the nation's most beloved desserts, and it doesn't get much more iconic than black and white cookies. I lived in Manhattan for six years during grad school and culinary school, and it's safe to say I had my share of black and white cookies, from famous bakeries to tiny bodegas. The easiest way to achieve the essential cake-like texture of black and white cookies? Cake mix! This shortcut eliminates a whole lot of measuring and scooping, leaving ample time for you to whisk up two silky-smooth glazes.

PREP	1 hour 25 minutes
COOK	15 minutes
Yield	*12 large cookies*

FOR THE COOKIES

2 (15.25-ounce) boxes vanilla cake mix

4 large eggs

1 cup vegetable oil

FOR THE GLAZES

2¼ cups confectioners' sugar

2 tablespoons milk, plus more as needed

1 tablespoon light corn syrup

2 tablespoons unsweetened cocoa powder

MAKE THE COOKIES In a medium bowl, stir together the cake mix, eggs, and vegetable oil. Cover the bowl with plastic wrap and refrigerate for 1 hour.

Preheat the oven to 350°F. Line two baking sheets with parchment paper.

Remove the dough from the fridge. Using two spoons or a measuring cup, scoop out ⅓-cup portions of the dough and roll into balls. Arrange the balls on the baking sheets, spacing them at least 2 inches apart, then flatten them slightly.

Bake the cookies for 12 to 15 minutes, until pale golden. Remove from the oven and let cool on the baking sheet for 10 minutes, then transfer to a wire rack to cool completely.

MAKE THE GLAZES Sift the confectioners' sugar into a medium bowl. Stir in the milk and corn syrup, adding more milk as needed, ½ teaspoon at a time, until the glaze reaches the consistency of thick syrup.

Invert the cookies so that the flat sides are facing up. Spread half of the flat side of each cookie with the white glaze. Refrigerate the cookies for 5 minutes.

continued

Add the cocoa powder to the bowl with the remaining glaze. Stir in more milk as needed, ½ teaspoon at a time, until the glaze reaches the consistency of thick syrup.

Glaze the other half of each cookie with the chocolate glaze, then refrigerate the cookies until the glaze sets, about 5 minutes.

Serve immediately or store in an airtight container at room temperature for up to 3 days.

Peanut Butter–Chocolate Sandwich Cookies

What's better than one peanut butter cookie? Two peanut butter cookies sandwiched together with a rich chocolate filling. If you're the type of person who can't snack on a banana without a tub of peanut butter nearby, then this cookie recipe is for you. Mashed bananas in the batter provide moisture (read: soft and chewy cookies!) and a hint of fruity flavor. I've kept the filling simple, smooth, and luxuriously thick to ensure your cookies stay sandwiched together bite after bite.

PREP	40 minutes
COOK	15 minutes
Yield	*16 cookies*

FOR THE COOKIES

1½ cups all-purpose flour

1 teaspoon baking soda

½ teaspoon baking powder

½ teaspoon kosher salt

1 cup creamy peanut butter

½ cup (1 stick) unsalted butter, at room temperature

¼ cup white sugar

¾ cup packed brown sugar

1 large egg

½ cup mashed banana

1½ teaspoons vanilla extract

FOR THE FILLING

½ cup (1 stick) unsalted butter, at room temperature

1½ cups confectioners' sugar, sifted

½ cup unsweetened cocoa powder, sifted

¼ teaspoon kosher salt

2 tablespoons heavy cream

1 teaspoon vanilla extract

MAKE THE COOKIES In a medium bowl, whisk together the flour, baking soda, baking powder, and salt.

In the bowl of a stand mixer fitted with the paddle attachment, beat together the peanut butter, butter, white sugar, and brown sugar until light and fluffy, about 2 minutes. Add the egg, mashed banana, and vanilla extract and beat until combined. Add the flour mixture and beat just until combined.

Line two baking sheets with parchment paper. Spoon out 2-tablespoon mounds of the dough onto the baking sheets, spacing them at least 2 inches apart. Refrigerate the cookies for 30 minutes.

Preheat the oven to 350°F.

Bake the cookies for 12 to 15 minutes, until they are golden brown around the edges. Remove them from the oven and let cool for 5 minutes on the baking sheets before transferring to a wire rack to cool completely.

MAKE THE FILLING In the clean bowl of a stand mixer fitted with the paddle attachment, beat the butter on low speed until smooth. Add the confectioners' sugar, cocoa powder, and salt and beat until combined. With the mixer running, slowly add the cream and vanilla extract and beat, scraping down the sides as needed, until light and fluffy, about 2 minutes. Increase the speed to high and beat the filling an additional 2 minutes.

Spread or pipe a portion of the filling onto the flat side of half of the cookies. Place a second cookie atop each to form sandwiches and serve.

Skillet Chocolate Chip Cookie

Secret ingredient

Buttermilk

A funny thing happens when you add buttermilk to chocolate chip cookies: You get an unexpected touch of tanginess you never even knew was missing from the classic confection. The subtle sourness offsets the sweetness of your chocolate chips of choice. I vote for a mix of semisweet, milk, and dark chocolate chips *and* chunks to keep taste buds on their toes. Slice and serve the cookie in wedges or go family-style by piling a few scoops of ice cream on top and handing everyone a spoon to dig in. (*Pictured on the following pages, 232–233.*)

PREP	15 minutes
COOK	35 minutes
Yield	*6 to 8 servings*

3 cups all-purpose flour

1 teaspoon baking soda

½ teaspoon kosher salt

1 cup (2 sticks) unsalted butter, at room temperature, plus more for greasing skillet

1 cup white sugar

¾ cup packed light brown sugar

2 large eggs, at room temperature

½ cup buttermilk

2 teaspoons vanilla extract

2 cups chocolate chips or chunks

1 teaspoon large-flake sea salt

Ice cream, for serving

Preheat the oven to 350°F.

In a medium mixing bowl, whisk together the flour, baking soda, and salt.

In the bowl of a stand mixer fitted with the paddle attachment, cream together the butter, white sugar, and brown sugar until light and fluffy, about 2 minutes. Add the eggs, one at a time, beating until combined. Beat in the buttermilk and vanilla extract just until combined. Add the flour mixture and mix just until the dough comes together. Mix in the chocolate chips.

Grease a 12-inch cast-iron skillet with additional butter.

Scrape the dough into the skillet, spread it evenly, then sprinkle it with the sea salt.

Bake the cookie for 32 to 35 minutes, until it's barely cooked in the center and slightly crisped around the edges.

Transfer the skillet to a wire rack and allow it to cool for 10 minutes. Top with ice cream and serve warm.

**Skillet Chocolate
Chip Cookie
(recipe, page 231)**

Inside-Out Coconut Macaroons

Flip an Almond Joy candy bar inside out and add a hazelnut twist to arrive at these one-of-a-kind coconut macaroons. Rather than pipe the chocolate-hazelnut spread into the treats, I freeze it into nickel-size mounds, then tuck them inside the coconut mixture prior to baking. After a hot date in the oven, the spread melts back to its smooth state. The result is a crispy, toasted coconut shell and a creamy chocolate center, and it only took you six ingredients to get there!

PREP	45 minutes
COOK	22 minutes
Yield	*20 macaroons*

⅓ cup chocolate-hazelnut spread (such as Nutella)

1 (14-ounce) bag sweetened coconut flakes

1 cup sweetened condensed milk

1 teaspoon vanilla extract

¼ teaspoon kosher salt

2 large egg whites

Line a baking sheet with parchment paper or wax paper. Spoon the chocolate-hazelnut spread into a sealable plastic bag or piping bag. Snip off a corner of the plastic bag or the tip of the piping bag and pipe twenty 1-teaspoon mounds onto the baking sheet, spacing them 1 inch apart. Freeze the chocolate-hazelnut chips until solid, about 30 minutes.

Preheat the oven to 350°F. Line a baking sheet with parchment paper.

In a medium bowl, stir together the coconut, condensed milk, vanilla extract, and salt. In a separate medium bowl, whisk the egg whites with an electric handheld mixer or whisk until stiff peaks form. Gently fold the egg whites into the coconut mixture.

Using an ice cream scoop or two spoons, scoop 2-tablespoon portions of the coconut mixture onto the lined baking sheet, spacing them 2 inches apart. Then, working quickly, press a frozen chocolate-hazelnut chip into the center of each macaroon.

Bake for 18 to 22 minutes, rotating the pans halfway through, until the macaroons are golden brown on top and around the edges.

Remove the macaroons from the oven and allow them to cool for 5 minutes on the baking sheet. Transfer the macaroons to a wire rack to cool completely, then serve.

Funfetti Celebration Cake with Chocolate Buttercream

My mom, Noni, imparted much of her baking wisdom to me from a very early age, but if there's one tip I rely on more than the rest, it's to always include pudding mix and sour cream in my cakes. The secret ingredients work hand in hand to take the moisture and flavor to all-new highs. In this case, we're talking about three luscious layers of rainbow-studded cake sandwiched together with my ultimate chocolate buttercream frosting. That alone is reason to celebrate!

PREP	30 minutes
COOK	30 minutes
Yield	*10 to 12 servings*

FOR THE CAKE

Cooking spray

3⅓ cups cake flour

1 (3.4-ounce) package vanilla instant pudding mix

1 teaspoon baking powder

¾ teaspoon baking soda

½ teaspoon kosher salt

1 cup (2 sticks) unsalted butter, at room temperature

2 cups white sugar

4 large eggs, at room temperature

1 cup whole milk

½ cup sour cream

2 teaspoons vanilla extract

¾ cup rainbow sprinkles, plus more for topping

FOR THE CHOCOLATE BUTTERCREAM

4 cups confectioners' sugar

1½ cups unsweetened cocoa powder

½ teaspoon kosher salt

¾ cup (1½ sticks) unsalted butter, at room temperature

⅔ cup whole milk

2 teaspoons vanilla extract

MAKE THE CAKE Preheat the oven to 350°F. Grease three 8-inch cake pans with cooking spray. Line the pans with parchment paper, then lightly coat the parchment paper with cooking spray.

In a medium bowl, whisk together the flour, pudding mix, baking powder, baking soda, and salt. Set the bowl aside.

In the bowl of a stand mixer fitted with the paddle attachment, cream together the butter and white sugar until light and fluffy, scraping down the sides of the bowl as needed, about 2 minutes. Add the eggs one at a time, beating between each addition.

Add the milk, sour cream, and vanilla extract and beat just until combined, scraping down the sides of the bowl as needed. The mixture may curdle but will smooth out once the dry ingredients are added.

Add the dry ingredients in three increments, mixing between each increment just until combined. Stir in the rainbow sprinkles, then divide the batter evenly among the prepared cake pans.

continued

Bake the cakes for 25 to 30 minutes, until a toothpick inserted comes out clean. Remove the cakes from the oven and set the pans atop wire racks to cool completely.

MAKE THE BUTTERCREAM In a large bowl, sift together the confectioners' sugar, cocoa powder, and salt.

In the clean bowl of a stand mixer fitted with the paddle attachment, beat the butter on medium speed until smooth, about 1 minute. Add the confectioners' sugar mixture and beat until combined, scraping down the sides as needed. With the mixer on low speed, slowly stream in the milk and vanilla extract and beat until combined, scraping down the sides of the bowl as needed. Increase the speed to high and beat the frosting until it is light and fluffy, about 2 minutes.

To assemble the cake, remove the cake layers from the pans, discard the parchment paper, and trim the tops if needed to make them level. Arrange one cake layer on your serving plate, then top it with a layer of frosting. Add a second cake layer on top with another layer of the frosting. Add the final cake layer, then frost the sides and top of the cake. Decorate the cake with additional sprinkles, then slice and serve.

Raspberry Chocolate Sheet Cake

Secret
ingredient

Red Wine

Raspberries and chocolate have been my favorite dessert combination since I was a child. And while sheet cakes may be reminiscent of kids' birthday parties, I've elevated that winning combination into an elegant, adult dinner party–worthy dessert. Warming the red wine prior to adding it to the cake batter helps bloom the cocoa powder, which translates to intensely rich chocolate flavor. Similarly, reducing more red wine along with jam makes an ultimate addition to light and fluffy raspberry buttercream. Swirl on the frosting, then top it off with fresh raspberries for a truly chic sweet.

PREP	25 minutes
COOK	35 minutes
Yield	*18 servings*

FOR THE CAKE

Cooking spray

1¾ cups all-purpose flour

1 cup unsweetened cocoa powder

1½ teaspoons baking soda

¼ teaspoon kosher salt

½ cup (1 stick) unsalted butter, at room temperature

¾ cup white sugar

½ cup packed light brown sugar

3 large eggs, at room temperature

2 teaspoons vanilla extract

½ cup sour cream, at room temperature

¼ cup vegetable oil

1 cup dry red wine, such as pinot noir, hot (see Kelly's Note)

2 cups raspberries

1½ cups chocolate chips

FOR THE FROSTING

½ cup dry red wine, such as pinot noir

¼ cup seedless raspberry jam

1 cup (2 sticks) unsalted butter, at room temperature

3 cups confectioners' sugar, sifted

———

2 cups raspberries, for decorating

MAKE THE CAKE Preheat the oven to 350°F. Grease a 13x9-inch cake pan with cooking spray.

In a medium bowl, whisk together the flour, cocoa powder, baking soda, and salt. Set the mixture aside.

In the bowl of a stand mixer fitted with the paddle attachment, cream together the butter, white sugar, and brown sugar until light and fluffy, about 2 minutes. Add the eggs one at a time, beating between each addition, then add the vanilla extract, sour cream, and oil and beat just until combined.

Alternate between adding add the flour mixture and the hot wine in three increments, beating between each addition.

Fold in the raspberries and chocolate chips, then scrape the batter into the prepared pan.

Bake the cake for 28 to 32 minutes, until a toothpick inserted comes out clean. While the cake is baking, make the frosting.

MAKE THE FROSTING In a small saucepan set over medium heat, whisk together the red wine and

continued

raspberry jam. Bring the mixture to a boil, then reduce to a simmer and cook, stirring occasionally, until it is reduced to ¼ cup and the consistency of syrup, about 12 minutes. Set the syrup aside to cool completely.

In the clean bowl of a stand mixer fitted with the paddle attachment, beat the butter on medium speed until smooth. Add the confectioners' sugar and beat until combined, scraping down the sides of the bowl as needed. Reduce the speed to low, then slowly stream in the red wine syrup, beating until combined and scraping down the sides of the bowl as needed. Increase the speed to high and beat the frosting for 2 minutes, until it is light and fluffy.

Once the cake has cooled completely, top it with the frosting and raspberries, then slice and serve.

Kelly's Note ✳ *To heat up the wine, microwave it in 30-second intervals, or warm it in a saucepan on the stove until it is hot to the touch.*

Cream Cheese Pound Cake with Lemon Curd

While vanilla extract may be a pantry staple for most, almond extract doesn't often earn a spot on the cabinet shelf. The truth is, almond extract is a welcome substitute for vanilla extract in nearly all cakes, from chocolate to banana to citrus, which leads me to this cake's smooth and tangy accompaniment: fresh lemon curd. This versatile topping, sauce, and filling is also a welcome pairing with scones, muffins, waffles, and tarts.

PREP	2 hours 20 minutes (including chilling)
COOK	1 hour 30 minutes
Yield	*16 servings*

FOR THE LEMON CURD

2 teaspoons finely grated lemon zest

½ cup fresh lemon juice

½ cup sugar

2 large eggs

6 tablespoons unsalted butter, cubed

FOR THE POUND CAKE

Unsalted butter and all-purpose flour, for greasing the pan

1½ cups (3 sticks) unsalted butter, at room temperature

1 (8-ounce) package cream cheese, at room temperature

2 cups sugar

¼ cup sour cream

2 teaspoons almond extract

5 large eggs, at room temperature

3 cups all-purpose flour

1 teaspoon baking powder

¼ teaspoon kosher salt

MAKE THE LEMON CURD In a medium saucepan set over medium heat, whisk together the lemon zest, lemon juice, sugar, and eggs until combined. Whisk in the butter and cook, whisking constantly, until the mixture thickens enough to coat the back of a spoon, 6 to 8 minutes. Transfer the lemon curd to a bowl, then cover the surface with plastic wrap. Refrigerate until chilled, at least 2 hours.

MAKE THE POUND CAKE Preheat the oven to 325°F. Grease and lightly flour a 10- or 12-cup Bundt pan.

In the bowl of a stand mixer fitted with the paddle attachment, beat the butter and cream cheese on medium-high speed until smooth, about 2 minutes. Add the sugar and beat until smooth, about 1 minute. Add the sour cream and almond extract and beat until smooth, about 1 minute. Add the eggs one at a time, beating on low speed between each addition, just until combined.

Add the flour, baking powder, and salt and beat just until combined.

Transfer the batter to the prepared cake pan. Bake the cake for 70 to 80 minutes, until a toothpick inserted comes out clean and the cake is dark golden. Remove the cake from the oven and allow it to cool completely in the pan. Invert the pan onto a serving platter.

When ready to serve, slice the pound cake, then top each slice with a dollop of the lemon curd.

Banana Cake with Cream Cheese Frosting

Secret ingredient

Crushed Pineapple

My mom Noni's banana sheet cake is legendary in San Diego. It's dense, moist, loaded with banana flavor, and slathered with the best cream cheese frosting. While I'm not one to mess with perfection, I've updated her recipe to include a tropical twist in the form of crushed pineapple. I've also modified the sheet cake to make two luscious layers joined together with her sweet and tangy cream cheese frosting.

PREP	25 minutes
COOK	1 hour
Yield	*12 servings*

FOR THE BANANA CAKE

Cooking spray

1½ cups mashed ripe bananas

1 (8-ounce) can crushed pineapple, drained

3 cups all-purpose flour

1½ teaspoons baking soda

¼ teaspoon kosher salt

¾ cup (1½ sticks) unsalted butter, at room temperature

2 cups white sugar

3 large eggs, at room temperature

2 teaspoons vanilla extract

1 cup buttermilk

FOR THE CREAM CHEESE FROSTING

2 (8-ounce) packages cream cheese, at room temperature

¾ cup (1½ sticks) unsalted butter, at room temperature

1½ cups confectioners' sugar

1 tablespoon vanilla extract

MAKE THE CAKE Preheat the oven to 350°F. Grease two 9-inch round cake pans with cooking spray. Line the pans with parchment paper, then grease the parchment paper with cooking spray.

In a small bowl, stir together the mashed bananas and pineapple. Set aside. In a separate small bowl, whisk together the flour, baking soda, and salt. Set aside.

In the bowl of a stand mixer fitted with the paddle attachment, cream together the butter and white sugar until light and fluffy, about 2 minutes. Add the eggs one at a time, beating between each addition, then add the vanilla extract. Beat in the flour mixture alternating with the buttermilk. Fold in the mashed banana mixture.

Divide the batter between the two prepared cake pans. Bake the cakes for 55 to 60 minutes, until a toothpick inserted comes out clean. Remove the cakes from the oven and allow them to cool completely.

MAKE THE FROSTING In the clean bowl of a stand mixer fitted with the paddle attachment, cream together the cream cheese and butter until smooth. Add the confectioners' sugar and vanilla extract and beat until combined.

To assemble the cake, remove the cake layers from the pans and discard the parchment paper. Arrange one cake layer on a serving platter. Top it with half of the frosting. Arrange the second cake layer on top. Frost the top of the cake with the remaining frosting. Slice and serve.

Pumpkin–Chocolate Chip Snack Cake

Is it breakfast? Is it dessert? Is it a snack? Pumpkin cake studded with chocolate chips doesn't discriminate when it comes to the time of day. The absence of frosting makes this cake perfectly acceptable for enjoying at all hours, but I vote that it's best alongside a cup of coffee (morning or night). Similar to pumpkin bread, its flavor is more spicy than sweet, with a combination of warming pumpkin pie spice and an entire half-teaspoon of freshly cracked black pepper to tickle your taste buds.

PREP	15 minutes
COOK	35 minutes
Yield	*9 to 12 servings*

Cooking spray

2 large eggs

1 cup canned pumpkin puree

1⅓ cups sugar

⅓ cup vegetable oil

½ teaspoon vanilla extract

1⅔ cups all-purpose flour

1 teaspoon baking soda

½ teaspoon baking powder

2 teaspoons pumpkin pie spice

½ teaspoon kosher salt

½ teaspoon freshly cracked black pepper

1 cup semisweet chocolate chips, divided

Preheat the oven to 325°F. Grease a 9-inch square baking pan with cooking spray, then line it with parchment paper so that it hangs off two of the sides. Grease the parchment paper with cooking spray.

In a large bowl, whisk together the eggs, pumpkin puree, sugar, oil, and vanilla extract. Add the flour, baking soda, baking powder, pumpkin pie spice, salt, and pepper and stir just until combined. Fold in ⅔ cup of the chocolate chips, then transfer the batter to the prepared baking pan. Sprinkle the remaining ⅓ cup chocolate chips on top.

Bake the cake until a toothpick inserted comes out clean, 30 to 35 minutes.

Remove the cake from the oven and let it cool slightly before slicing and serving.

Carrot Cupcakes with Cream Cheese Frosting

Secret ingredient

Chocolate

There's only one thing my boys love more than playing in the dirt: eating cupcakes. As long as they're going to be loading up on sugar, I might as well sneak some veggies in there, too. Classic carrot cupcakes get a subtle chocolate spin with the addition of cocoa powder, which blends in seamlessly with the cinnamon-spiced and crushed pineapple–studded cake batter. But the real draw here for my tiniest of taste testers is the cream cheese frosting, crushed chocolate cookie "dirt" and candy melt "carrots." This is one type of dirt I don't mind them eating!

PREP	1 hour 10 minutes
COOK	25 minutes
Yield	*18 cupcakes*

FOR THE CARROT CUPCAKES

3 cups peeled and grated carrots

1½ cups all-purpose flour

½ cup unsweetened cocoa powder

2 cups white sugar

1 teaspoon baking powder

½ teaspoon baking soda

1 teaspoon ground cinnamon

½ teaspoon kosher salt

4 large eggs

½ cup vegetable oil

2 teaspoons vanilla extract

1 (8-ounce) can crushed pineapple, drained

FOR THE FROSTING AND DECORATIONS

1 cup orange candy melts

1 cup green candy melts

2 (8-ounce) packages cream cheese, at room temperature

1 cup (2 sticks) unsalted butter, at room temperature

1½ cups confectioners' sugar, sifted

2 teaspoons vanilla extract

½ cup finely crushed chocolate wafers or sandwich cookies

MAKE THE CUPCAKES Preheat the oven to 350°F. Line 18 cups of two 12-cup muffin pans with cupcake liners.

In a large bowl, combine the grated carrots, flour, cocoa powder, white sugar, baking powder, baking soda, cinnamon, and salt. In a separate medium bowl, whisk together the eggs, oil, vanilla extract, and crushed pineapple. Add the wet ingredients to the dry and stir just until combined.

Divide the batter among the muffin cups, filling each cup three-fourths full. Bake the cupcakes for 20 to 25 minutes, until a toothpick inserted comes out clean.

Remove the cupcakes from the oven and set aside to cool completely.

MAKE THE FROSTING AND DECORATIONS Line a baking sheet with parchment or wax paper.

In two separate bowls, melt the candy melts in the microwave in 30-second intervals, stirring between each interval, until smooth. Transfer the melted

continued

orange candy to a sealable plastic bag or piping bag and the green candy to a separate bag. Snip off an ⅛-inch corner of the bag with the orange candy, then pipe 18 carrot shapes onto the baking sheet. Snip off an ⅛-inch corner of the bag with the green candy, then pipe green stems atop each carrot. Set the decorations aside to harden completely.

In the bowl of a stand mixer fitted with the paddle attachment, beat together the cream cheese and butter until smooth, about 2 minutes. Add the confectioners' sugar and vanilla extract and beat until smooth.

Slather or pipe the frosting atop the cupcakes. (If piping, refrigerate the frosting for 15 minutes before transferring to a sealable plastic bag and snipping off the corner.) Top the frosting with the crushed chocolate wafers.

Using an offset spatula, carefully release the carrot decorations from the baking sheet. Insert a carrot into the frosting on each cupcake and serve.

Fudgy Brownie Tart

Warning: This recipe is not for the chocolate faint of heart. It combines the best elements of three beloved desserts: the chocolatey flavor of brownies, the gooey center of lava cake, and the creamy consistency of pudding. It all comes together into one big, crustless tart. A splash of Kahlúa liqueur introduces a hint of coffee, with intense chocolate flavor stretching from the jiggly center to the barely set edges. This brownie pudding-pie is best served with a scoop of slow-melting vanilla ice cream by its side.

PREP	10 minutes
COOK	12 minutes
Yield	*12 servings*

Cooking spray and all-purpose flour, for greasing the pan

¾ cup (1½ sticks) unsalted butter

10 ounces semisweet chocolate, chopped

¼ teaspoon kosher salt

2 teaspoons vanilla extract

3 large eggs

2 large egg yolks

¼ cup coffee liqueur (such as Kahlúa)

1 cup confectioners' sugar, plus more for serving

½ cup all-purpose flour

Vanilla ice cream, for serving

Preheat the oven to 425°F. Grease and flour a 9-inch tart pan with a removable bottom.

In a large microwave-safe bowl, combine the butter and chocolate. Microwave in 30-second increments, stirring as needed, until melted. Whisk in the salt and vanilla extract. Whisk in the eggs, egg yolks, and liqueur, then whisk in the confectioners' sugar and flour just until combined.

Pour the batter into the tart pan, then place it on a baking sheet. Bake the tart for about 12 minutes, until it is set but still slightly jiggly in the center. Remove the tart from the oven and allow it to cool completely.

Remove the sides of the tart pan. Dust the top of the tart with confectioners' sugar, slice into wedges, and serve with vanilla ice cream.

Salted Caramel Bread Pudding

Chocolate Croissants

With a house full of hungry boys, our bread cabinet is fully stocked at all times with sliced loaves for turkey sandwiches, homemade tortillas for breakfast burritos, and chocolate croissants for indulgent treats. Despite a high turnover rate, I'm always on the verge of one carb or another nearing expiration. Thankfully, stale carbs are bread pudding's best friend. The drier the bread, or in this case, chocolate croissant, the more custard it absorbs. So buy in bulk and don't let a single carb go to waste!

PREP	25 minutes
COOK	35 minutes
Yield	*8 servings*

FOR THE SALTED CARAMEL SAUCE

½ cup white sugar

3 tablespoons unsalted butter, cubed and at room temperature

¼ cup heavy cream

½ teaspoon kosher salt

FOR THE BREAD PUDDING

Unsalted butter, for greasing the pan

5 large eggs

1 cup whole milk

1 cup heavy cream

½ cup white sugar

¼ cup packed light brown sugar

1 tablespoon vanilla extract

½ teaspoon kosher salt

8 large chocolate croissants, cut into 1-inch cubes (see Kelly's Note)

MAKE THE SAUCE Heat the white sugar in a medium saucepan set over medium heat, occasionally stirring with a rubber spatula, until the sugar begins to clump together, about 3 minutes. Continue stirring constantly until the clumps dissolve and the sugar turns dark golden brown in color, an additional 2 to 3 minutes.

Immediately add the butter and stir to combine. While whisking, slowly stream in the cream; it will bubble vigorously. Boil the mixture, undisturbed, for 1 minute. Remove the caramel from the heat, then stir in the salt. Set the sauce aside to cool slightly; it will thicken as it cools.

MAKE THE BREAD PUDDING Preheat the oven to 350°F. Grease a 13x9-inch baking dish with butter.

In a large bowl, whisk together the eggs, milk, cream, white sugar, brown sugar, vanilla extract, and salt. Add the croissant cubes and fold together the ingredients until combined.

Pour the croissant cubes and all liquid into the baking dish. Cover the dish with plastic wrap and set aside for 30 minutes to allow the croissants to soak up the custard. Alternately, refrigerate the bread pudding overnight.

Preheat the oven to 350°F.

Bake the bread pudding until set and the croissants begin to crisp slightly on top, about 30 minutes. (If baking straight from the refrigerator, bake for an additional 10 to 15 minutes.)

Remove the bread pudding from the oven and let cool for 20 minutes.

Serve the bread pudding drizzled with the salted caramel sauce.

Kelly's Note ⁎ *If your chocolate croissants are fresh, cube them, then scatter on a baking sheet and toast in a 350°F oven until they are slightly crisped. Let cool slightly before continuing with the recipe as directed.*

Key Lime Cheesecake Bars

One of the first times I ever visited my husband's home state of Florida, we had dinner at Joe's Stone Crab, a Miami Beach institution since 1913. The legendary eatery is known for its seafood dishes and is also home to one of my husband's favorite desserts, Joe's Famous Key Lime Pie. One taste, and I was also hooked. I've re-created the pie in cheesecake bar form, adding toasted coconut to the classic graham cracker crust. It's no Joe's, but it's certainly husband-approved!

PREP	3 hours 20 minutes
COOK	30 minutes
Yield	*9 to 12 bars*

Cooking spray

9 sheets graham crackers

1 cup sweetened coconut flakes, divided

3 tablespoons unsalted butter, melted

1 (14-ounce) can sweetened condensed milk

1 (8-ounce) package cream cheese, at room temperature

2 teaspoons grated Key lime zest

½ cup Key lime juice

1 large egg

Whipped cream, for serving

Preheat the oven to 350°F. Line an 8-inch square baking pan with foil, then grease the foil with cooking spray.

In a food processor, pulse the graham crackers until they are roughly ground. Add ½ cup of the coconut flakes and continue pulsing until the graham crackers are finely ground.

In a medium bowl, stir together the graham cracker mixture and melted butter. Transfer the mixture to the prepared pan and press firmly into an even layer on the bottom.

In the bowl of a stand mixer fitted with the paddle attachment, beat together the condensed milk, cream cheese, lime zest, and lime juice until well combined. Beat in the egg. Pour the cheesecake mixture atop the crust, spreading it into an even layer.

Bake the cheesecake for 20 to 25 minutes, until the center is almost set. Remove the cheesecake from the oven and let it cool completely before covering the pan with plastic wrap and refrigerating for 3 hours.

When ready to serve, toast the remaining ½ cup coconut in a small skillet set over medium heat, stirring frequently, until golden brown and crunchy, about 3 minutes. Set the coconut aside to cool completely.

Remove the cheesecake from the fridge, then slice it into bars. Top each bar with a dollop of whipped cream and a sprinkle of the toasted coconut, then serve.

Quick Apple Turnovers

Secret ingredient

Gruyère Cheese

Turnovers that flirt with the line between savory and sweet are the best kind of turnovers. These flaky pockets are home to the conventional pairing of tangy green apples, brown sugar, and ground nutmeg. That's where the familiar stops and the new kids enter the pastry party. Nutty Gruyère cheese and fresh thyme balance out the fruity sweetness of the caramelized apples. While Gruyère is my cheese of choice, sharp cheddar and even Brie would be welcome swap-ins. The more melting power, the better. (*Pictured on the following pages, 256–257.*)

PREP	20 minutes
COOK	20 minutes
Yield	*8 turnovers*

2 cups small-diced cored peeled Granny Smith apples (2 medium apples)

⅔ cup shredded Gruyère cheese

2 tablespoons brown sugar

1 tablespoon chopped fresh thyme

¼ teaspoon ground nutmeg

All-purpose flour, for dusting work surface

1 (17.3-ounce) package frozen puff pastry (2 sheets), thawed

1 large egg, beaten with 1 tablespoon water

Demerara cane sugar, for topping

Preheat the oven to 400°F. Line two baking sheets with parchment paper.

In a large bowl, stir together the apples, Gruyère, brown sugar, thyme, and nutmeg.

Lightly flour your work surface, then unfold the puff pastry sheets. Using a rolling pin, roll over the pastry to seal any perforations, then cut each sheet into 4 squares.

Spoon the apple mixture into the center of each square, dividing it evenly. Fold one edge of each square pastry across diagonally to form triangles. Using a fork, crimp the edges to seal, then transfer the turnovers to the prepared baking sheets, spacing them at least 2 inches apart.

Cut three small slits in the tops of each turnover, then brush with the egg wash. Sprinkle with the cane sugar.

Bake the turnovers for 17 to 20 minutes, until golden brown and puffed. Remove the turnovers from the oven and let cool slightly before serving.

Quick Apple
Turnovers
(recipe, page 255)

Strawberry Galette with Whipped Cream

The first time I tasted strawberries with balsamic vinegar was at the Fishery in Pacific Beach, California, a seafood market and restaurant with a surprisingly stellar dessert menu. The marriage of sweet fruit and sour vinegar hit all the flavor high notes. I've put this duo, plus a bit of fresh rosemary, to work inside a flaky, free-form galette crust. A second secret ingredient makes its debut in my go-to homemade whipped cream, which gets shine and tang from sour cream.

PREP	1 hour (including chilling)
COOK	45 minutes
Yield	*6 servings*

FOR THE DOUGH

1¾ cups all-purpose flour, plus more for rolling out dough

1½ tablespoons minced fresh rosemary

1 tablespoon white sugar

½ teaspoon kosher salt

¾ cup (1½ sticks) cold unsalted butter, cubed

3 tablespoons ice water

FOR THE FILLING

4 cups quartered strawberries

3 tablespoons white sugar

1 tablespoon cornstarch

1 tablespoon balsamic vinegar

___

1 large egg, beaten with 1 tablespoon water

Demerara cane sugar, for topping (optional)

FOR THE WHIPPED CREAM

1 cup heavy cream

⅓ cup sour cream

¼ cup confectioners' sugar

2 teaspoons vanilla extract

MAKE THE DOUGH In the bowl of a food processor, combine the flour, rosemary, white sugar, and salt. Add the cubed butter and pulse until the mixture resembles wet sand. With the motor running, slowly stream in the ice water, 1 tablespoon at a time, until the dough begins to form a ball.

Shape the dough into a disk and wrap it securely in plastic wrap. Refrigerate for 30 minutes while you prepare the filling.

MAKE THE FILLING In a large bowl, stir together the strawberries, white sugar, cornstarch, and balsamic vinegar. Set the filling aside.

Preheat the oven to 350°F. Line a baking sheet with parchment paper.

Lightly flour your work surface. Remove the dough from the fridge, then using a rolling pin, roll into a 14-inch round. Drape the dough around your rolling pin and transfer it to the baking sheet.

Using a slotted spoon, transfer the filling into the center of the dough, leaving a 2-inch border around

continued

the edges. Using your fingers, fold the edges of the dough up and over the filling. Brush the top of the dough with the egg wash, then sprinkle it with cane sugar if desired.

Bake the galette for 40 to 45 minutes, until the crust is golden brown and the filling is bubbly. Set the galette aside to cool completely while you make the whipped cream. (The juices in the galette will thicken as it cools.)

MAKE THE WHIPPED CREAM In the bowl of a stand mixer fitted with the whisk attachment, beat together the heavy cream, sour cream, confectioners' sugar, and vanilla extract until medium peaks form.

Slice the galette into wedges, then top with whipped cream and serve.

Mix-and-Match Berry Hand Pies

I started making dessert hand pies in 2012, when the trend made a resurgence after years outside the food magazine spotlights. I dabbled with caramel-apple and strawberry-chocolate variations before settling on mixed berry as my handheld pie of choice. Vodka had been my not-so-secret weapon over the years for the flakiest, most tender pie crust. I noticed another bottle in my liquor cabinet had the same proof *and* was more flavorful, so it was Grand Marnier for the win! Fruit and citrus are always a winning duo, no matter how you mix and match them. Swap in whatever berries, apples, pears, or stone fruits look best at your local market.

PREP	1 hour 25 minutes (including chilling)
COOK	15 minutes
Yield	*10 hand pies*

FOR THE PIE DOUGH

2 cups all-purpose flour

½ teaspoon kosher salt

½ teaspoon baking powder

¾ cup (1½ sticks) cold unsalted butter, cubed

¼ cup vegetable shortening

¼ cup orange liqueur (such as Grand Marnier), chilled

2 to 3 tablespoons ice water

FOR THE FILLING AND TOPPING

1 cup diced berries

¼ cup white sugar

1½ teaspoons all-purpose flour

1 teaspoon fresh lemon juice

¼ teaspoon ground cinnamon

2 large egg yolks

1 tablespoon heavy cream

Demerara cane sugar (optional)

MAKE THE PIE DOUGH In a food processor, pulse together the flour, salt, and baking powder until combined. Add the butter and shortening and pulse until the mixture resembles wet sand. Add the liqueur and 2 tablespoons ice water and pulse just until the dough comes together. If the dough appears too dry, add additional ice water, 1 teaspoon at a time, as needed.

Transfer the dough to your work surface and shape into a 6-inch disk. Wrap the dough securely in plastic wrap and refrigerate until firm, a minimum of 1 hour, or up to overnight.

MAKE THE FILLING Preheat the oven to 425°F. Line two baking sheets with parchment paper.

In a medium bowl, stir together the berries, white sugar, flour, lemon juice, and cinnamon. Set the filling aside.

Generously flour your work surface. Unwrap the dough and using a rolling pin, roll it into a 14-inch round. Using a 3-inch round cookie cutter, cut out

continued

as many rounds as possible. Re-roll the scraps and continue cutting out rounds until you run out of dough. You should have approximately 20 rounds. (See Kelly's Notes.)

Arrange half of the rounds on the baking sheets, spacing them at least 2 inches apart. Using a slotted spoon, divide the filling among the centers of the dough, leaving a ½-inch border around the edges. Place a second dough round on top of the filling. Use a fork to crimp together the top and bottom dough rounds to seal the pies shut.

In a small bowl, whisk together the egg yolks and cream. Brush the tops of the hand pies with the egg wash. Sprinkle the hand pies with the cane sugar, if desired. Use a sharp knife to cut three small slits in the top of each hand pie.

Bake the hand pies until golden brown, about 15 minutes.

Remove the hand pies from the oven and transfer to a wire rack. Serve warm or at room temperature.

Kelly's Notes * *Hand pies can be made in any shape or size, from rounds and half-moons to triangles and rectangles. If you don't have a cookie cutter, use a sharp knife to trace your shape of choice.*

Frozen fruit can be used in this recipe, however it should be fully thawed and drained of any excess liquid to avoid soggy hand pies.

Chocolate Shell Ice Cream Topping

My mom, Noni, grew up in Gary, Indiana, where her after-school snack of choice was a Dairy Queen chocolate-dipped cone. Fast-forward a generation, and my siblings and I have inherited her same love of Dairy Queen, seeking out the nearest franchise wherever we are to enjoy that satisfactory snap of the first bite into a hard chocolate shell. The only thing better is the cool and creamy vanilla soft serve that waits beneath. Now, we re-create the nostalgic sweet with our chocolate(s) of choice, plus a modern-day upgrade of a pinch of ground ginger and salt.

PREP	5 minutes
COOK	1 minutes
Yield	*1 cup*

8 ounces chocolate (see Kelly's Note), chopped

3 tablespoons coconut oil (measured in the liquid state)

1½ teaspoons ground ginger

¼ teaspoon kosher salt

Ice cream, for serving

In a medium microwave-safe bowl, combine the chocolate and coconut oil. Microwave in 30-second intervals, stirring between each interval, until melted.

Stir in the ginger and salt and serve over your favorite ice cream.

Kelly's Note ✳ *Any combination of semisweet, bittersweet, or dark chocolate will work well in this recipe.*

Ice Cream Pie Template

Ice Cream Cones

Every time I buy ice cream cones, I open the box and am met with a handful of intact cones and a whole lot more broken pieces. When life gives you shattered cones, make ice cream pie! Both waffle and sugar cones are easily transformed into pie crust, but I prefer the buttery flavor of the waffle variety. It's only the first of several decisions you'll be making when using this ultimate ice cream pie template. Get creative with your ice cream flavors and toppings, because the combinations are truly endless.

PREP	6 hours 20 minutes (including freezing)
COOK	10 minutes
Yield	*8 servings*

1¼ cups finely crushed waffle or sugar cones (see Kelly's Note)

4 tablespoons unsalted butter, melted

3 tablespoons sugar

6 cups ice cream(s) of your choice

½ cup chopped toppings of your choice, such as candy, sprinkles, cookies, or nuts

1½ cups whipped cream, for serving

Chocolate sauce or caramel sauce, for serving

Preheat the oven to 350°F.

In a medium bowl, stir together the crushed waffle cones, butter, and sugar until combined. Press the mixture firmly into the bottom and up the sides of a 9-inch metal pie plate.

Bake the crust for 10 minutes, then set it aside to cool completely. Remove the ice cream from the freezer to soften slightly while the crust cools.

Once the crust has cooled, add alternating layers of the ice cream and your choice of toppings into the crust. Wrap the pie securely with several layers of plastic wrap, then freeze it until frozen solid, a minimum of 6 hours.

When ready to serve, remove the plastic wrap and top the pie with the whipped cream. Slice and serve with your choice of sauce.

Kelly's Note ∗ *The ice cream cones must be finely crushed so that they can be tightly packed into the pie plate to form the crust.*

Adults-Only Milkshakes

Secret ingredient

Cabernet Sauvignon

I love my wine as much as the next mom of three kids under age five. Now you can drink your wine and eat it, too. Reducing an entire bottle of red wine down to a single cup yields an intense, fruit-forward syrup that gives fudge and caramel a run for its milkshake-making money. Customize the consistency of your shake by adding more or less milk to thin it to your preferred texture.

PREP	1 hour
COOK	1 hour
Yield	*4 to 6 milkshakes*

1 (750-ml) bottle cabernet sauvignon

1 cup sugar

1 (1½-quart) carton vanilla ice cream

2 cups whole milk, plus more as needed

Blackberries, for serving

In a medium saucepan set over medium heat, whisk together the wine and sugar. Bring the mixture to a boil, then reduce to a simmer and cook until it begins to foam and has reduced to 1 cup, about 1 hour. Set the wine syrup aside to cool completely; it will thicken as it cools.

In a blender, combine the ice cream, milk, and ¾ cup of the wine syrup. Blend until creamy.

Drizzle the remaining wine syrup around the insides of the serving glasses. Pour the milkshake into the glasses, top with blackberries, and serve immediately.

Dinner Party Crème Brûlée

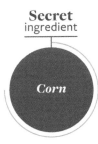

Corn

If an elegant sweet finale is your goal, then crème brûlée is your dessert. The smooth custard and crackly sugar topping are notoriously finicky to make, which is why you may have restricted this dish to a restaurant-only indulgence. I've streamlined the process and made it possible to whip up this fine-dining dessert a day or two in advance. Corn lends an earthy sweetness and can be used in fresh or frozen form, which means party-worthy crème brûlée can be on your dinner table 365 days a year.

PREP	1 hour 30 minutes
COOK	48 minutes
Yield	*8 servings*

1 tablespoon unsalted butter

1 cup fresh or thawed frozen corn kernels

4 cups heavy cream

6 large egg yolks

1 cup sugar, divided

1½ teaspoons vanilla extract

● **EQUIPMENT**
Kitchen torch

Preheat the oven to 325°F.

Combine the butter and corn in a medium saucepan set over medium-low heat. Cook, stirring occasionally, until the butter is melted and the corn is tender, about 8 minutes. Add the cream and bring the mixture to a boil, then turn off the heat and let it sit for 10 minutes. Transfer the mixture to a blender and puree until smooth.

In a medium bowl, whisk together the egg yolks with ½ cup of the sugar and the vanilla extract. Slowly stream the corn mixture into the bowl, whisking constantly. Strain the mixture through a fine mesh sieve.

Arrange eight (6-ounce) shallow ramekins in two shallow baking pans. Divide the mixture among the ramekins, then transfer the pans to the oven. Using a pitcher, pour water into the pans to reach halfway up the sides of the ramekins.

Bake the crème brûlées for 35 to 40 minutes, until they are set in the center and no longer jiggly. Remove from the oven and set aside to cool completely.

Sprinkle the crème brûlées with the remaining ½ cup sugar, then use a kitchen torch to caramelize the tops. Serve immediately.

Kelly's Note ✳ *To make the crème brûlées in advance, prepare them up through the point where you set them aside to cool. Cover securely with plastic wrap and refrigerate for up to 1 day. When ready to serve, bring them to room temperature, then proceed to caramelize the tops.*

Drinks

The V.I.P.

The V.I.P. cocktail and I have a storied history that dates back to the 2010s at Del Frisco's steakhouse in midtown Manhattan. The restaurant's signature martini stars vodka-infused pineapple, hence the name "V.I.P." Over time, it turned into my celebratory drink of choice for work promotions and other special occasions. The cocktail became a symbol of good luck and good times for our family, so much so that my husband and I chose it as the signature drink at our wedding in Los Angeles, nearly six years after we shared our first V.I.P. cocktail in New York City. A sliced vanilla bean lends subtle sweetness and warming aromatics to this tropical sipper.

PREP	2 days
COOK	None
Yield	*4 cocktails*

16 ounces (2 cups) vodka

2 cups diced pineapple

1 vanilla bean

In a bowl, combine the vodka and pineapple.

Slice the vanilla bean in half lengthwise and scrape the seeds into the bowl. Stir to combine and add the vanilla bean pod. Cover the bowl securely with plastic wrap and refrigerate for a minimum of 48 hours, or up to 1 week.

When ready to serve, strain the vodka and discard the pineapple and vanilla bean pod.

To make one cocktail, add 4 ounces of the pineapple-infused vodka to a cocktail shaker filled with ice. Cover and shake vigorously, then strain the mixture into a glass and serve.

Kelly's Note * *Do not be tempted to eat the post-vodka-soak pineapple. It will be very bitter and unpleasant tasting since the vodka has extracted all of its flavor and sweetness.*

La Jolla Sunset

I love a good fruity cocktail, the kind that goes down easy and leaves you dreaming of a warm ocean breeze. But mixing up an adult spin on fruit punch requires disguising the flavor of alcohol without creating an overwhelmingly sweet concoction that puts you on the bus to Hangover City. I've layered vodka, peach schnapps, and orange juice with tangy pomegranate juice to create an ombré sunset. The drink is named after my hometown of La Jolla, California, known as "The Jewel," and pomegranate seeds are the perfect garnish, sparkling like tiny rubies atop your drink.

PREP	5 minutes
COOK	None
Yield	*1 cocktail*

1½ ounces vodka

½ ounce peach schnapps

2 ounces orange juice

2 ounces pomegranate juice

1 tablespoon pomegranate arils

Fill a serving glass with ice. Add the vodka, peach schnapps, orange juice, and pomegranate juice, in that order, then garnish with pomegranate arils and serve.

Pitcher Bloody Marys

When it comes to brunchtime cocktails, I am staunchly in the mimosa camp. I generally go for bubbly and fruity over spicy and tomatoey. But add pickles to the equation and my allegiance will quickly turn. The salty brine cuts the acidity of tomato juice, while a pinch of sugar lends a little sweetness to your glass. Best of all, this mix can be whipped up a day in advance, then topped off with vodka right before serving. Don't forget the pickles, bacon, and celery garnishes for dipping and dunking!

PREP	30 minutes
COOK	None
Yield	*4 to 6 cocktails*

3 cups tomato juice

½ cup pickle juice

2 tablespoons Worcestershire sauce

2 tablespoons fresh lemon juice

2 teaspoons fresh horseradish

4 dashes hot sauce

1 tablespoon sugar

¼ teaspoon black pepper

8 ounces (1 cup) vodka

Pickles, celery, and bacon, for garnish

In a large pitcher, combine the tomato juice, pickle juice, Worcestershire, lemon juice, horseradish, hot sauce, sugar, and pepper. Cover and refrigerate for a minimum of 30 minutes, or up to overnight.

When ready to serve, stir in the vodka. Fill servings glasses with ice, then pour in the mixture. Garnish with pickles, celery, and bacon and serve.

Cucumber Mojito

Secret ingredient

Lemongrass

My husband, Julio, isn't usually a fan of sugary cocktails, but he'll make an exception for a mojito. I've swapped out the sugar for honey and avoided sweetness overload with the addition of lemongrass. If you've never tasted fresh lemongrass, it has hints of both tangy citrus and fresh mint. Discard the tough, woodsy stalks and use only the inner core, which you'll muddle with cucumber and lime for a refreshing fusion of Cuban and Asian flavors.

PREP	5 minutes
COOK	None
Yield	*1 cocktail*

2 lemongrass stalks (core only), cut into thin slices

1 (2-inch) piece cucumber, peeled

¼ cup honey

3 fresh mint leaves, plus more for garnish

¼ lime

2 ounces white rum

Club soda

In a cocktail shaker, combine the lemongrass, cucumber, honey, mint, and lime. Muddle the mixture together until the cucumber is completely mashed and the lemongrass is bruised.

Add the rum and enough ice to fill the shaker. Cover and shake vigorously. Fill a cocktail glass with ice. Strain the mixture into the glass, then top it off with club soda, garnish with mint, and serve.

Melon Ball Sangria

Basil

I'm saying goodbye to sangria with sliced fruits and rounding out the mix with melon balls, and not just any melon balls. The trio of watermelon, cantaloupe, and honeydew spheres get a little extra love thanks to a soak in orange liqueur and a quick stop in the freezer. Ice cubes need not apply for this party-in-a-pitcher that's sweetened with homemade basil simple syrup.

PREP	25 minutes
COOK	None
Yield	*4 cocktails*

¼ cup sugar

1 cup fresh basil leaves

¼ cup water

8 watermelon balls

8 cantaloupe balls

8 honeydew melon balls

4 ounces (½ cup) triple sec (such as Cointreau)

1 (750-ml) bottle prosecco

In a small saucepan set over medium heat, combine the sugar, basil, and water. Bring the mixture to a boil, then remove from the heat. Let the basil simple syrup cool completely, then strain and refrigerate until needed.

Combine the watermelon, cantaloupe, and honeydew balls in a large bowl. Pour in the triple sec and stir to combine. Using a slotted spoon, arrange the melon balls in a single layer on a parchment paper–lined baking sheet. (Reserve the triple sec left in the bowl.) Freeze the melon balls for a minimum of 15 minutes, or up to 1 day.

In a pitcher, combine the basil syrup, frozen melon balls, reserved triple sec, and prosecco. Stir the mixture, then pour into glasses and serve.

Boozy Iced Coffee

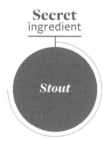

Stout

What do you get when a Vietnamese iced coffee meets an Irish Slammer? Boozy iced coffee! If the idea of caffeinated beer makes you think twice, allow me to coax you into whipping up this cocktail with the reassurance that this recipe has passed the taste test with many a beer-averse (myself included). The combination of coffee, stout, and Irish whiskey, along with a swirling ribbon of sweetened condensed milk, makes for a flavor-packed blend that will certainly kick your senses (and you) into high gear.

PREP	5 minutes
COOK	None
Yield	*1 drink*

4 ounces brewed coffee, chilled or at room temp

2 ounces stout, such as Guinness

1 ounce Irish whiskey

2 teaspoons brown sugar

1 ounce sweetened condensed milk

In a serving glass, stir together the coffee, stout, whiskey, and brown sugar.

Add ice to fill the glass. Add the sweetened condensed milk and serve.

Spiced Strawberry Margarita

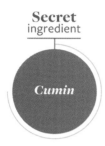
Practically every Mexican restaurant in Southern California lays claim to the region's best margarita. It's been my unofficial duty to test those claims, from Javier's in Century City, Los Angeles, to Puesto in Seaport Village, San Diego. I've drawn inspiration from all the way down the 101 freeway to bring the spice cabinet to your cocktail glass. A toasted-cumin simple syrup lends smoky flavor to sweet strawberries and an anything-but-classic margarita mix.

PREP	30 minutes
COOK	None
Yield	*1 cocktail*

1½ teaspoons cumin seeds

½ cup water

½ cup sugar

3 strawberries, halved

¾ ounce fresh lime juice

2 ounces silver tequila

Lime wedge, for lining rim

Tajín seasoning, for lining rim

Heat the cumin seeds in a small saucepan set over medium heat, stirring occasionally, until toasted and fragrant, about 1 minute.

Add the water and sugar to the pan, whisking to combine. Bring the mixture to a simmer and cook until thickened slightly, about 20 minutes. Remove from the heat and let cool completely. Strain out the seeds and set the cumin simple syrup aside.

In a cocktail shaker, muddle together the strawberries and lime juice. Add the tequila and ¾ ounce of the cumin syrup. Fill the shaker with ice, cover, and shake vigorously.

Rub the lime wedge around a fourth of the rim of the serving glass, then dip it in the Tajín. Fill the glass with ice, then strain the mixture into the glass and serve.

Kelly's Note ✳ *Store extra simple syrup in an airtight container in the fridge for up to 1 week.*

Hot Chocolate

Secret ingredient

Chai Spices

I didn't start drinking coffee until my mid-20s, so my original coffee shop order of choice was a chai tea latte. Fast-forward a decade and I've combined my love of chai spices with my kids' love of hot chocolate. The combination of cocoa powder, five toasty spices, and a splash of vanilla extract makes this a warming concoction that's anything but basic. For the 21+ crowd, try adding a shot of Kahlúa, Baileys, or brandy for extra kick. (*Pictured on page 285.*)

PREP	10 minutes
COOK	5 minutes
Yield	*1 drink*

1 cup whole milk

3 tablespoons sugar

1½ tablespoons unsweetened cocoa powder

¼ teaspoon ground ginger

⅛ teaspoon ground allspice

⅛ teaspoon ground cinnamon

⅛ teaspoon ground cardamom

⅛ teaspoon ground cloves

½ teaspoon vanilla extract

Whipped cream, for serving

In a medium saucepan set over medium heat, whisk together the milk, sugar, cocoa powder, ginger, allspice, cinnamon, cardamom, and cloves. Cook, stirring occasionally, until the mixture is warm, about 5 minutes.

Remove the mixture from the heat. Whisk in the vanilla extract, then pour into a mug. Top with whipped cream and serve.

Hot Chocolate
(recipe, page 283)

Black and Blue

If you're looking for a cocktail that doesn't taste like a cocktail, allow me to introduce you to the Black and Blue. Muddled berries, fresh citrus, and sugar work their magic to disguise the taste of gin. However, the real hero here is a final splash of nonalcoholic ginger beer, whose carbonation has a way of camouflaging the taste of liquor. The warm, slightly spicy taste of ginger in this fizzy, fruity cocktail will win over even the biggest of gin cynics.

PREP	5 minutes
COOK	None
Yield	*1 cocktail*

5 blackberries, plus more
for garnish

10 blueberries

¼ lemon, plus a slice for garnish

1 tablespoon sugar

2 ounces gin

Ginger beer

In a cocktail shaker, muddle together the blackberries, blueberries, lemon, and sugar. Add the gin, then fill the shaker with ice. Cover and shake vigorously.

Fill a serving glass with ice. Strain the mixture into the glass, then top with ginger beer. Garnish with additional whole blackberries and a slice of lemon and serve.

index

NOTE: Page references in *italics* indicate photographs.